P9-DHK-597

# Recipes from the French Kitchen Garden

# Recipes from the French Kitchen Garden

BRIGITTE TILLERAY

PHOTOGRAPHED BY DAVID GEORGE

CASSELL

*To Christian,*
*my one and only seed of life,*
*with love and pride*

First published 1995 by
Cassell Publishers Ltd
Wellington House
125 Strand
London WC2R 0BB



Distributed in the United States by
Sterling Publishing Co. Inc.
387 Park Avenue South, New York, NY10016-8810

Distributed in Australia
by Capricorn Link (Australia) Pty Ltd
2/13 Carrington Road
Castle Hill
NSW 2154

**British Library Cataloguing-in-Publication Data**
A catalogue record for this book is available
from the British Library.

ISBN 0-304-34383-8



Designed by Isobel Gillan
Illustrations by Diana Leadbetter
Typeset by Litho Link Ltd, Welshpool, Powys, Wales

Printed and bound in Singapore

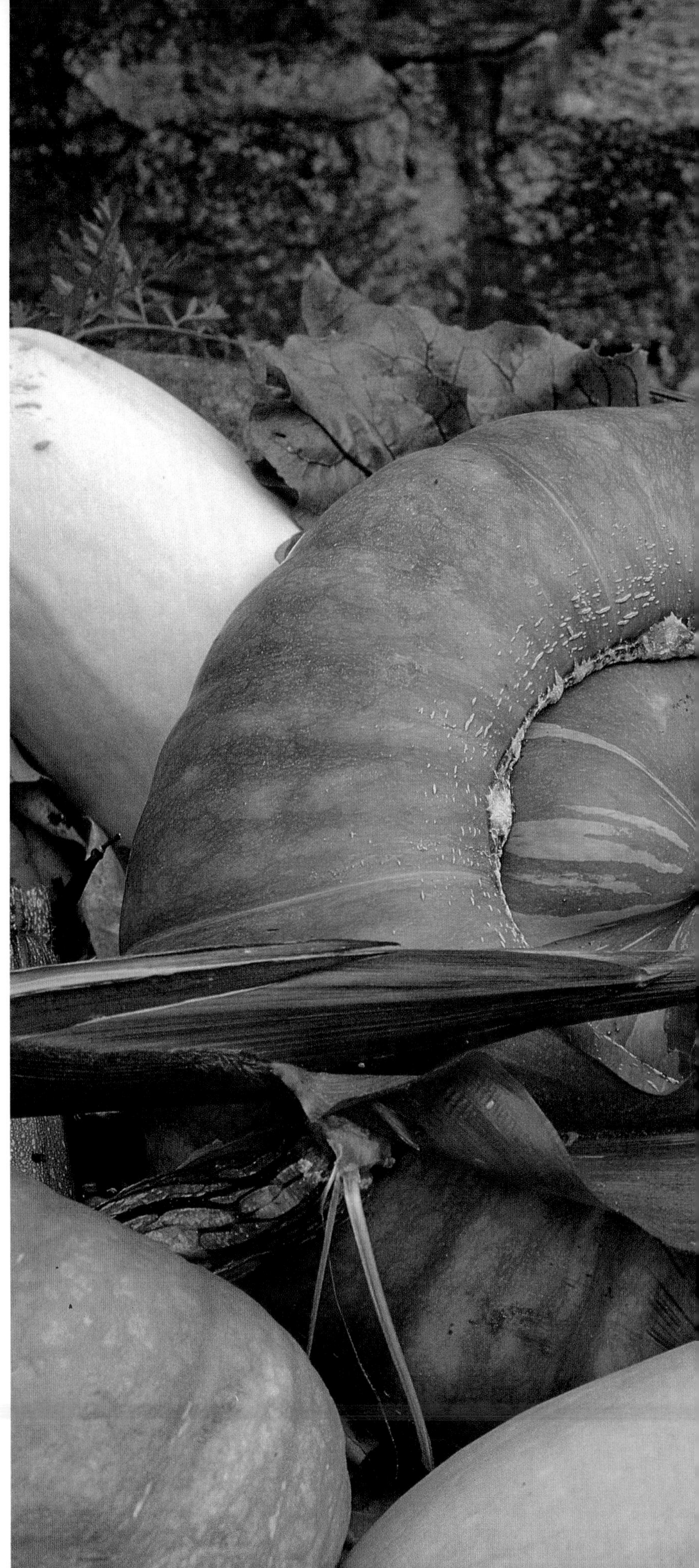

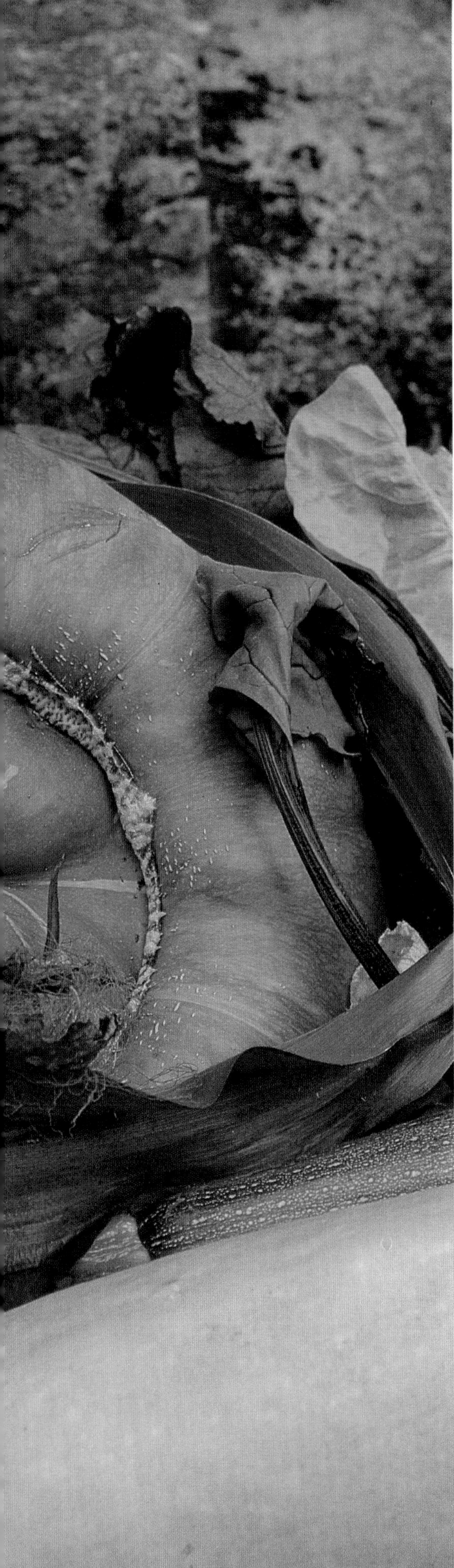

# Contents

# Acknowledgements

My thanks go to all those of my compatriots, passionate gardeners, who have spared time to pass on their knowledge of fruit and vegetable gardening, a skill and way of life inherited from their forefathers and rooted in ancient civilizations.

My thanks, too, for the use of many kitchens and the disclosure of so many delicious recipes.

Finally, thank you, David, for having focused yet again, with such sensitivity, on another facet of the Frenchwoman: her art of bringing self-sufficiency to the table.

*Garden produce and preserves, stored in the cellar.*

# *Introduction*

A walk through today's French garden provides vivid proof of the inextricable link, in the Frenchman's mind, between his land and the preparation of food: fruit and vegetables take precedence over flowers and shrubs grown for ornament. Small or on a grander scale, the carefully cultivated kitchen garden has its place around every French home.

For the layman, the various species may be seen only in terms of their nutritive qualities, but in fact, each one, from the humble cabbage to the sun-gorged melon, has a long and fascinating history. It evokes the mythology of our civilization, reminds us of the great explorers and their expeditions, of human endeavour and superstitions which surrounded the arrival of each new species in Europe. It speaks volumes about the evolution of mental and social attitudes.

In France, the gardener and the agronomist are blessed by the diversity of the soil and climate. Species which have to be grown under glass in other countries, ripen naturally in France, season by season, region by region, providing us with an astounding range of healthy and delicious produce.

The ever-changing variety of herbs, fruit and vegetables makes its own unique contribution to the culinary kaleidoscope which in France finds its way daily straight from the garden to the table.

*A typical potager provides fruit and vegetables all the year round*

# Le Potager

*Laelian with prize-winning courgettes*

The French kitchen garden had humble origins. The very word *potager* signified a few modest plants grown around the house to add goodness to the *potage*, the daily brew which, with a small amount of meat, was the French peasant's main source of nourishment from time immemorial.

Then suddenly, as new fruit and vegetable species were brought back from abroad by the king's messengers, the French attitude towards the *potager* was totally revolutionized.

Pragmatism gave way to hedonism and, at vast expense, the vegetable and fruit gardens of the châteaux of France were landscaped and manicured so that kings, queens, ambassadors and visitors could enjoy the sight of orderly exotica as well as the culinary preparations which ensued.

By the mid-seventeenth century, the *potager* had become a passion; La Quintinie, for example, left the serious profession of the law to become the royal gardener at Versailles. Le Potager du Roi and the gardens of the château of Villandry became the most copied kitchen gardens of France amongst the aristocracy. Petits pois and peaches were served fresh in December, together with small beans and strawberries, and summer-houses erected at the centre of vegetable beds became the venue for serious political meetings.

*Sunflowers brought back from the allotment.*

By the end of the eighteenth century, vegetable, herb and fruit gardens were to be found throughout France. Often entwined with flowers, the *potager*, groomed by the gardener or tended lovingly by the owner, flourished under French skies, paying off with abundant yield throughout the seasons.

By the end of the nineteenth century, for those not blessed by a country or town garden, a liberal Catholic priest, l'Abbé Lemire, created the first allotments, so that the factory or office worker could supplement his modest salary by growing food for his family. Lemire wrote:

> To complement industrial work, the allotment will give the worker a knowledge of his personality. It will give him a sense of leisure by doing work that he enjoys. It will help him to measure and deploy his physical strength. By his own efforts man will create beauty which must be the eternal and gratifying start to moral ascension.

# The French Vegetable Garden

For a long time in Europe, the only leguminous addition to meat soups and stews came from the gathering of wild leaves.

It was not until the seventeenth century that the cultivation of vegetables became fashionable in France. Surrounded by walls to protect the new-found plants from prowlers, vegetables supplied the kitchens of the wealthy and the humble alike. Thus was the French kitchen garden born.

From then on the consumption of vegetables increased, encouraged by the publication of food and gardening manuals. A whole new generation of revered gardeners and agronomists appeared. Extensive new species were created and the de Vilmorin family sold their first catalogue of vegetable seeds. Every layman's dream was to have his small cottage surrounded by a vegetable and fruit plot.

Things have not changed much today, and given a small piece of land, the French countryman will prefer to plant vegetables rather than flowers. The sight of leeks growing in a modest front garden may invite the foreign visitor to smile at such true French pragmatism, but it is only the result of a long history of social order, a tangible need to nurture and create. Every Frenchman knows that passionate and constant work in the well-groomed kitchen garden will feed his family throughout the year.

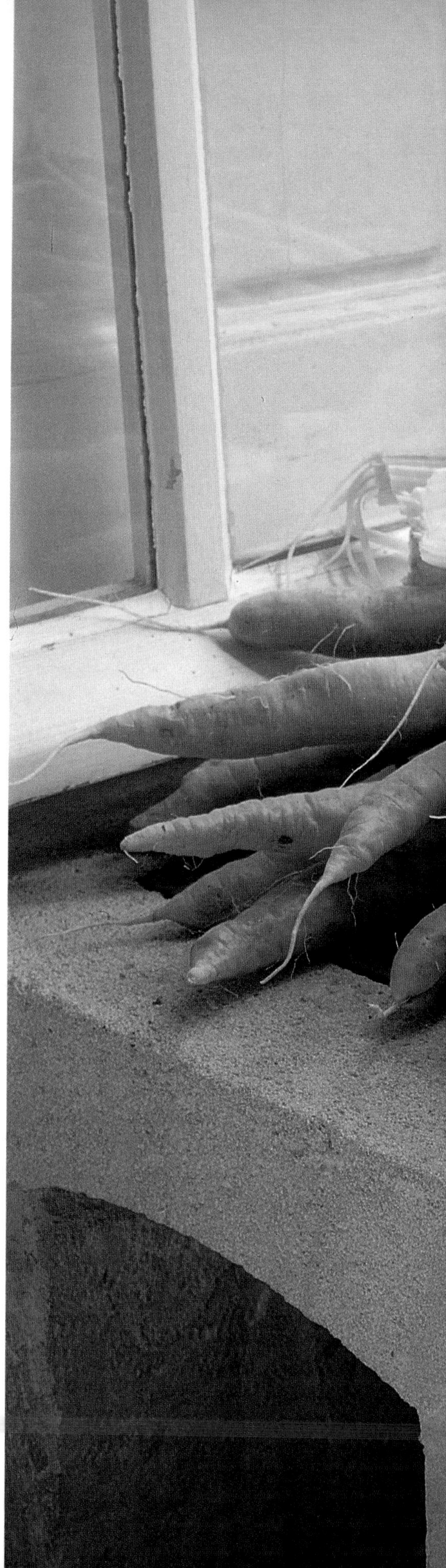

*From the old kitchen potager, vegetables have been gathered for the potée*

But that is not all. There is currently a great revival of interest in home-grown vegetables at all levels of French society. A fad? Maybe: but, above all, yet another illustration of the French discernment for quality in food and awareness of new diets and of varieties which cannot be found on the open market. Tired of imported exotica, French gardeners are exchanging seeds, bartering plants and re-creating a *potager* full of the flavours of yesteryear, with succulent species which had long been forgotten.

## *Ail*

GARLIC

A universal ingredient in French cooking, garlic grows in most Southern gardens.

Virgil and Aristophanes referred to the medicinal virtues of the plant for athletes and farmworkers and today it is still prescribed as a cure for blood disorders, high cholesterol and the common cold.

*Drying garlic in the Provence sun*

If the flavour of pink or purple garlic such as the Rosé de Lautrec is quite pungent, the large-cloved white variety is milder, especially when fresh. For better digestion, always discard the small green shoot at the centre of each clove.

Garlic is used in sauces, marinades and herb butter, and to stud legs of French lamb and pork. But the true flavour explodes when garlic is pounded in a mayonnaise to make *aïoli,* a condiment served in Provence with myriad steamed and raw vegetables, cold meat, poultry, fish and seafood.

When cooked – boiled or grilled – garlic becomes sweet and the taste is relatively subtle. A clear soup made with garlic boiled in consommé, a hint of basil and a few peeled tomatoes is a delicate summer first course. Try baking a guinea-fowl in a covered earthenware crock with twenty or more unpeeled garlic cloves, a few lardons and a glass of crisp white wine . . . two hours later, the garlic has caramelized and taken on the buttery flavour of the fowl. Served with a green salad, the meat is succulent and the garlic can be peppered, spread on thin pieces of toast and served as croûtes.

Gather garlic from early summer onwards. Dry the heads in full sun and keep in bunches in a dry, well-aired place.

## *Artichaut*

ARTICHOKE

The French discovered the art of eating artichokes when the high-spirited young Queen Catherine de Medicis had them brought to the French garden from Italy in the sixteenth century.

The Queen was said to be so fond of the vegetable that she ordered little pastries filled with artichoke hearts and cockerel combs to be served with every meal at Court.

A *field of artichokes in Provence*

Today, this handsome thistle lavishly adorns most kitchen gardens. In spring-time in Provence, the little violet artichoke, Violet de Provence, appears first. Young and tender, before the chokes have formed, it will be eaten *à la poivrade,* sliced raw in a vinaigrette sauce. More advanced, it will be simmered *à la barigoulde* with a herby filling of garlic and parsley. As the season ripens into summer, larger varieties such as the Camus de Bretagne burgeon in the gardens of Britanny, the Loire Valley and Normandy.

Eating artichokes is a homely ritual. The leaves are peeled off the cold vegetable one by one and dipped in a plain vinaigrette dressing, or a *ravigote* sauce made with a strong mustard, or a *gribiche,* the delightful French dressing made with oil, vinegar and a touch of strong mustard, chopped hard-boiled egg, chives, chervil, tarragon and capers. Then the hairy choke is removed and more sauce is spooned into the centre of the artichoke heart.

In Normandy, artichokes are eaten warm as a first course, with a light cream and butter sauce. At the height of the season, the leaves are often discarded altogether and the heart filled with a *salpicon,* a mixture of other spring vegetables such as peas and chopped chives with melted butter, and used to garnish roast meat. Tender peas cooked with spring onions and tiny lardons make a fine filling.

Braised *à l'ancienne* with a veal and anchovy filling, the artichoke becomes a wholesome

*An antique French asparagus dish*

summer main course. But once mixed with delicate oyster mushrooms and made into a buttery soufflé, it is transformed into a culinary *chef-d'œuvre.*

Artichokes will grow in most gardens until the first frost. Once the choke has been allowed to turn to a deep purple flower, it can be picked and dried for winter flower arrangements.

## *Asperge*

ASPARAGUS

Wild asparagus grows on Mediterranean soil. Slender and pale, it has a remarkable flavour and is lauded to the skies by the great chefs. Heralding elegant summer luncheons, the cultivated tips, green or purplish-white, large or slender, according to the variety appear throughout France from May onwards.

The fine flavour of this vegetable is regarded with due respect, and a place apart on the menu is always reserved for asparagus. In the South, it is steamed or boiled until just tender, then dipped while still hot in a sauce made with oil, lemon juice and chopped chervil or simply seasoned with salt and pepper. North of the river Loire, cream and butter sauce prevails as an accompaniment. Served hot with the asparagus, it complements the taste without impairing it.

With Sunday summer brunch becoming more and more fashionable, asparagus tips are dipped into freshly boiled eggs or served steamed, as a side dish, with fluffy, truffled scrambled eggs.

An effective diuretic, rich in fibre and an excellent stimulant to the digestive system, asparagus is high on the list of *cuisine minceur.*

## *Aubergine*

AUBERGINE

The aubergine originated in Burma, and was first grown in Italy in the fifteenth century. In France, it first appeared in the *potager* at Versailles when Louis XIV, eager to emulate the Italians, demanded that *melanzana* should be served at royal banquets.

One of the main ingredients of ratatouille, aubergine grows best in Provence or the South-West, where the huge Violette Ronde or the white-fleshed Violette de Toulouse reaches full size. Although low in calories, the soft flesh can absorb an enormous amount of oil. Therefore, it is recommended that the vegetable should be sliced and sprinkled with salt and left to stand for 30 minutes before cooking. It will then retain less oil while cooking.

Aubergine can be baked with onions, tomatoes and cheese or stuffed *à la niçoise* with a meat or vegetable stuffing. Cut into fine strips, lightly floured and deep-fried, it makes a featherweight fritter to be served piping hot, with a spicy tomato sauce. As a first course, it can be sliced and marinated in fruity olive oil, lemon and garlic and makes a delectable and fragrant ragoût when simmered with spring lamb.

Along with *caviar d'aubergine,* a delicious smoky purée of the grilled vegetable mixed with olive oil, lemon juice and garlic, there are traditional recipes of Mediterranean family cooks such as salads made with ripe tomatoes, slices of cold grilled or fried aubergines, topped with local cheeses and olives. But chefs have started to approach aubergine with more sophistication and full respect for its fine consistency. Today, aubergine is often steamed and made into a light soufflé, or puréed with a touch of basil, revealing the delicate texture and flavour of this vegetable.

## *Bette*

SWISS CHARD

The main ingredient of French soups in the Middle Ages, *bette* or *blette*, according to the region, has thick white ribs and large, shiny green leaves. Stalks and leaves are eaten separately.

In Burgundy and Lyon, the white ribs are first blanched with lemon juice, then mixed with a thick white sauce and baked into a golden gratin.

The leaves are used in the preparation of more esoteric recipes, some of which can be ascribed to

*Sprinkled with olive oil, a simple first course of aubergine, tomato and fresh cheese*

the Moors or the Crusaders. In the Vaucluse and Provence chard leaves are used to make *gayette,* a light flat sausage mainly eaten cold. The leaves can also be wrapped round meat balls which are then baked in a *provençale* sauce into tender *paupiettes.*

An original speciality of Auvergne is the *pounti,* a savoury *clafoutis* or batter pudding, made with chopped chard leaves, bacon and prunes. A robust dish, it is served on its own as a first course.

Typical of the traditional recipes of Nice is the *tarte de blette,* a substantial dessert and inspired mixture of sweet and savoury flavours: the chard leaves are blanched and chopped, then mixed with apples, sultanas soaked in rum, *eau-de-vie,* pine nuts and finely grated Parmesan cheese. The mixture is baked in a sweet pie crust. Sprinkled with icing sugar, it is eaten cold or lukewarm.

## *Betterave*

BEETROOT

Believed to originate from the banks of the Caspian Sea, beetroot was introduced to France in the sixteenth century by the revered agronomist, Olivier de Serres.

Like most root vegetables, it is a precursor of winter dishes and spicy soups, but the small round salad variety can be picked as early as July. The more flavoursome *crapaudine,* a longish root, is an autumn vegetable. Indigenous of Alsace and the North, it is worth seeking out.

In Normandy, summer beetroot is grated raw in a creamy vinaigrette and added to a potato, chive and smoked herring salad.

Cold cooked beetroot is the constant companion of grated carrots and other cooked or salad vegetables in all platters of *crudités.* Mixed with walnuts and chicory, it makes the archetypal Christmas salad.

Served hot, beetroot is a useful addition to any autumn menu. Thick slices sautéed in garlic butter are served with brown rice for a vegetarian main course. Lightly caramelized in orange butter, it is excellent with roast game. In Picardy, homeland of *soubise* – onion – sauce, beetroot is sliced and seasoned with *soubise* as an accompaniment to roast pork.

Sliced wafer-thin and then deep-fried, beetroot makes unusual crisps to serve with drinks.

Beetroot will keep throughout the winter months, if stored in sand away from the frost.

## *Cardon*

CARDOON

This large edible thistle is grown in all the kitchen gardens of Provence, to be served as a separate course during the traditional Christmas Eve meal.

The preparation is fairly time-consuming. The large ribs have to be stripped off their spikes, then carefully blanched in water, lemon juice and flour. This way, they will stay perfectly white before being simmered in a luxurious sauce made with cream and truffles, or with cream, garlic and anchovies.

In Lyon, cardoons are blanched then baked with a fine *salpicon* of shallots and bone marrow.

The finest variety is the Cardon de Tours, with an especially delicate taste. For keen kitchen gardeners only.

## *Carotte*

CARROT

One of the very few vegetables indigenous to Europe, in France the pink flower of the wild carrot still adorns our summer hedgerows.

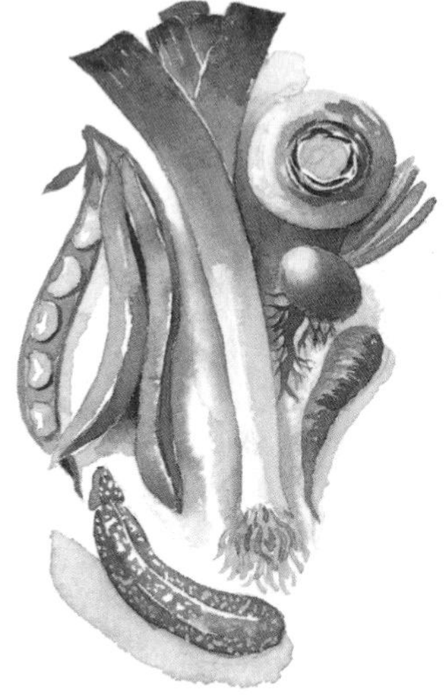

*The Frenchman's garden: an inextricable link between his land and the preparation of food*

Until the Dutch produced in the seventeenth century the first orange species that we know today, the carrot was white and scrawny, with a slightly bitter taste. Today, it is a joy to pick this sweet vegetable from the garden from early spring and so until the first winter frost.

Of the best known French varieties – there are over twenty – Carotte Grelot is tiny and sweet and a good garnish for meat. The larger Carotte Nantaise is probably the best known.

The carotene found in this root vegetable is the most natural precurrent of vitamin A. It is good for the skin and the digestion and is prescribed in many diets – hence *carottes Vichy*, a dish of plainly boiled carrots first served to patients in the renowned spa town of the Auvergne.

In French cooking, the use of the carrot is endless. Puréed, it is delicately laced with cream in *potage Crécy*. Alternatively, mixed with onions, potatoes and leeks, it becomes the colourful ingredient of solid country soups, *pot-au-feu*, *daubes*, sauces and marinades.

New carrots are good on their own, cooked with herbs. The addition of a tangy orange butter gives carrots a distinctive flavour when served with grilled or roast meat.

Diced carrot plays its part in the vegetable medley, *macédoine de légumes*, mixed with other young vegetables. The same mixture features in a traditional dish of the Loire Valley, succulently glazed in the cooking juices of a piece of veal casseroled with white wine.

Raw and grated, freshly picked carrots make a simple first course tossed in vinaigrette with parsley or chervil. Mash the yolk of a softly boiled egg in the vinaigrette or add a few chopped black olives and coriander leaves to the dressing.

*Vegetables ready to be cleaned in the garden shed*

In the Nivernais, a sweet pie is made with grated carrots, ground almonds, brown sugar, eggs and rum, baked in a pastry crust and served lukewarm. It is a cousin of the *tartouillat* of the Sologne, which is made with pumpkin.

To add a *nouvelle cuisine* touch, prepare carrot butter to serve with a light celeriac mousse (for recipe see page 124).

## *Céléri*

CELERY

Wild celery – lovage – used to grow wild throughout Europe and was commonly used to flavour the food of the Egyptians, the Greeks and the Romans. It was only in the seventeenth century that the Italians began cultivating celery and its large root, celeriac. Both stalks and root are rich in a highly aromatic oil which gives the vegetable its very distinctive taste.

The young stalks and leaves, chopped and tossed in a mustardy dressing, are often eaten as an appetizer in French homes. They can also be cooked in boiling water and served with meat juices, béchamel or Mornay sauce, or baked in a gratin like Swiss chard.

Celeriac is eaten raw as a winter salad. It is also grated and stirred into a *rémoulade* sauce made with cream and mustard. All French *charcuteries* offer it for sale next to the grated carrots.

But it is during cooking that the perfumed, smoky flavour of this vegetable emerges. Diced and boiled, it can be glazed in the cooking juices of roast chicken, turkey or guinea-fowl.

Cooked in chicken stock, then puréed with butter and cream, celeriac makes what must be regarded as the finest of winter soups, topped with toasted almonds. When stuffed with country ham and cheese, then baked slowly in the oven, celeriac becomes an unusual main course.

Celeriac will keep like any other root vegetable, in a dry place, away from the frost.

*The cabbage, the staple diet of rural France*

## *Chou*

CABBAGE

The oldest indigenous vegetable of Europe, cabbage is grown from the North to the Mediterranean. For a long time, it was one of the main staples of the rural diet. It fed centurions under the Roman Empire and soldiers during the 100 Years War, and has kept both rich and poor in good health throughout history.

Rich in vitamins C, and A, B and K, cabbage also has a high mineral content and is low in calories. An antiseptic, it drains the digestive system, is good for the skin and known to revitalize the whole body.

As well as an immense variety of green, white and red cabbages, the *Brassica* family also includes the cauliflower, first grown in Italy with its cousin, broccoli, and the swede, known in France under its Latin name, *rutabaga,* as well as the kohlrabi, *chou-rave.*

The French brassica harvest depends on location, variety and time of year. The Savoy cabbage retains the first dew drops of spring, whilst the giant Naples cabbage and the brussels sprout will tolerate the winter frosts.

In cooking, cabbage is traditionally the indispensable ingredient of *potée, soupe au chou, garbure,* and other regional variations of dishes with roborant virtues. Other classic cabbage dishes include *chou farci,* a stuffed cabbage, *chou rouge au lard,* red cabbage with bacon and apples, and, of course, *choucroute,* the pickled cabbage of Eastern France, which is so good for the health despite the copious quantities of pork products which normally accompany it.

All good solid food, but there is more to the cabbage than that. In the eighteenth century the illustrious chef Carême created the fine art of wrapping fowl and game in cabbage leaves to make succulent little moulds: *chartreuse.* Today, aware of the savour and originality that the leaf confers, chefs use cabbage in exquisite and unusual combinations, always crisp, colourful and still packed with its natural goodness.

## *Courge*

GOURD

The *Cucurbita* family is considerable. From the mighty pumpkin to the tiny gherkin, gourds inhabit the earth with dinosaurian unconventionality. Some handsome, some ugly, some smooth, some gnarled, some perfect, some crimson, some pale . . . all are capped by a delicate calycular flower.

If gourds have inspired the painter, the potter and the ceramist, they should do likewise for the cook. Their shape is conducive to the presentation of food. Their flesh, somewhat timid both in taste and consistency, lends itself to refined mixtures and culinary conspiracies.

Squash and marrows are delicious with a meat or vegetarian stuffing. Courgettes are so good that all they require is to be simply steamed and seasoned with butter or olive oil and fresh coriander. They can of course be prepared in *tian,* a Provençal gratin where they are baked with rice and grated cheese, or in layers with tomatoes and cheese. Stuffed with meat, fish or rice, they can also accompany other small vegetables in *petits farçis niçois.* Courgettes make light fritters with Corsican mint, and are pleasant grated into summer salads.

Of the same family, cucumber is the ideal accompaniment to cold or smoked fish. The vegetable can be scooped out and filled with cream cheese and anchovies or fromage blanc and smoked salmon. Always sprinkle a touch of fresh dill on the surface.

Melons need to be very ripe and can be served on their own with a liqueur or some other summer fruit.

In Normandy, a sweet custard tart is made with the cooked pulp of pumpkins. In the Sologne and the North, the same custardy mixture is salted and served warm in a savoury tart as a first course. But the most wholesome recipe for pumpkin must be one I shared with friends in a mountain chalet last winter. Cut a large lid off the top of the pumpkin. Discard seeds and fibres. Fill the cavity with a mixture of country bread generously rubbed with garlic, sliced wild mushrooms, thick cream and grated Gruyère, Comté or Beaufort cheese,

*Still life with gourd*

seasoned with a touch of oregano, a pinch of nutmeg and plenty of black pepper. Replace the lid and tightly wrap the whole pumpkin in a double layer of baking foil. Place in a bain-marie and bake in a low oven (150°C / 325°F / gas mark 3) for 3 hours. When the lid is finally opened, the soft pumpkin flesh will have melted with the other ingredients and simply needs to be spooned out. With it we drank chilled flowery Alsace wine. It was gustative bliss.

*Shallots drying on the garden step*

## Échalote

SHALLOT

A wild species from Ascalon, in Palestine, this cousin of the onion was brought back to France by the Crusaders.

A precious source of vitamins B and C, shallot is chopped raw in salad dressings, and served with vinegar as a sauce for oysters.

In cooking, it is the base of many sauces: *béarnaise, bercy* and the delicate *beurre blanc nantais* which goes so well with perch or salmon.

Among the French varieties, look for the large Cuisse de Poulet, which is firm, full of flavour, and will keep for months in a dry place.

## Épinard

SPINACH

Another trophy of the Crusaders, spinach is one of the first spring vegetables. Among a few French varieties, the wide-leaved Monstrueux de Viroflay is mild and tangy and does not melt down too much in cooking.

The keen spinach gardener will add two other varieties to his collection. First, *rumex patientia*, more commonly known as everlasting spinach. It has the advantage of resisting the frost and produces good-sized leaves all year round. The other species is just making a comeback on the list of old-fashioned vegetables. It is the orach Roi Henri which grows wild in the valleys of the Alps.

Spinach has a good vitamin C and iron content, but should not be kept long after cooking, for it ferments rapidly.

Young raw shoots make a good *salade tiède,* or warm salad, when mixed with potatoes which have been sautéed with onions, garlic and bacon, or wild mushrooms.

Cooked spinach makes a fine soup and soufflé. Baked in a tart with a Mornay sauce, it is a useful standby for impromptu lunches. As a side vegetable, it is often served with white meat, simply buttered, although children will find it more palatable mixed with crème fraîche or a smooth béchamel sauce.

True spinach devotees will want to try this surprisingly good winter pudding, *épinards au sucre*. Blanch the spinach, then drain well, making sure all the cooking liquid has run out. Purée in a food mill and mix with good unsalted butter, a pinch of freshly grated nutmeg and soft brown sugar to taste. Pile the spinach purée in a dome shape on to a warmed serving platter. Bring a good amount of crème fraîche to boiling point, adding a teaspoon of finely grated lemon zest and a touch of brown sugar. Pour the cream, piping hot, over the spinach purée and serve with croûtons of sponge cake fried in butter.

## Fenouil

FENNEL

A Mediterranean plant introduced to France in the sixteenth century, fennel needs sun and grows mainly in Provence.

*Long fennel stalks will be used for barbecuing fish*

The stalks are highly decorative in the kitchen garden and should be dried into twigs for barbecuing fish. The seeds give a pleasant taste to vinegar. The bulb has a mild aniseed taste and can be chopped raw into a mixed salad, as follows: choose small fennel bulbs and keep some of the leaves. Quarter each bulb and mix the fennel pieces with cherry tomatoes, a few artichoke hearts, a young courgette, sliced, a dozen quail's eggs and a few leaves of oak-leaf lettuce. To make the dressing, mash chopped black olives with 2 anchovy fillets, olive oil, lemon juice and salt and pepper to taste. Mix into the salad and serve with toasted bread rubbed with garlic and olive oil.

Cooked, fennel is a mild green vegetable which makes an excellent accompaniment to roast chicken, pork, veal and steamed white fish. Baked with chopped tomatoes, olive oil and herbs, it takes on the flavours of the Mediterranean and complements a dish of barbecued sea bass or any white fish.

## BROAD BEAN

At a time when only wild herbs and leaves entered the cooking pot, broad beans were already in use as a vegetable. The first detailed record of the broad bean in Europe was in Great Britain between 1000 and 500 BC.

In France, implanted by the Emperor Charlemagne, it featured in ancient recipes for soups, stews and a dish of fish with onions and saffron. In the nineteenth century, the broad bean was classed as peasant food by the French bourgeoisie, who found it indigestible and a source of flatulence. Little did they know that it would make such a fashionable comeback with *nouvelle cuisine.*

Today, in Provence, the first broad beans of May are served raw, *á la croque au sel* – simply with sea salt. This brings out the fresh nutty flavour and the beans are good with the first outdoor drinks.

In cooking, it is a rule of thumb to blanch the broad beans, once podded, for 3–5 minutes, according to size. Remove the outer skin of each bean, which will enable you to appreciate the true flavour and will also prevent the beans from being indigestible. With young broad beans, try this old Provençal recipe, *pasta fresca aï faveta*: blanch the beans and remove the outer skins, then boil until just tender. Drain them well and toss into fresh tagliatelle with chopped peeled tomatoes, garlic, olive oil and basil.

Large broad beans can be cooked in well-flavoured chicken broth with summer savory or sage. Alternatively, rosemary flavours broad beans well. Whatever the choice of herb, the beans can then be seasoned with white or tomato sauce, or puréed into a soup. Serve with small pieces of ham diced on top.

## Haricot

BEAN

Brought into Europe by Christopher Columbus, this species of bean is very prolific. There are five main varieties in the French garden: the dwarf bean, *haricot vert,* which is the finest, then the dwarf mange-tout, *haricot mange-tout,* which contains tiny haricot beans. Another variety, *haricot beurre,* is pale yellow. We then find the trailing mange-tout, among which Princesse à Rame is a great French favourite. All these varieties are eaten whole. Finally, there is a choice of dwarf and trailing haricot beans which may be eaten podded, as soon as the envelope starts drying on the plant. The remaining harvest is bunched up and kept hanging in a cool, dry place to be used dried for winter meals.

*The haricot bean, the main ingredient of Napoleon's favourite dish*

The dwarf green bean such as the Petit Gris is delicate and best picked almost as the cooking water comes to the boil – a kitchen gardener's privilege. Enhance the flavour with just a small knob of butter and a light sprinkling of parsley. For a light summer first course or a cold accompaniment to rabbit terrine try this salad. Cook and drain the green beans. Mix them with cherry tomatoes, a good vinaigrette dressing and a few coriander leaves. Toast some pine nuts in a frying pan and sprinkle over the salad. Children, who are so often reluctant to try plain green vegetables, usually like green beans served with *tomates provençales,* sliced tomatoes quickly fried in oil with basil and garlic.

The green mange-tout bean can be prepared in much the same way. Once again, try not to impair the fine flavour.

Napoleon's favourite dish was a warm salad of fresh haricot beans, tossed in thick, fruity olive oil, lemon juice and garlic. This recipe has stayed on the menus of Provence, whilst in Normandy, freshly boiled haricot beans are laced with thick cream, seasoned with parsley and simmered over a low heat.

A solid carbohydrate, it often takes the place of potatoes in soups. An essential ingredient of *cassoulet,* the robust dish of goose or duck, pork and beans served in Toulouse and throughout the South-West, the haricot bean is also cooked into a delectable *ragoût* with lamb. In South Britanny, the same *ragoût* is made with tuna fish, tomatoes and white wine, while in Burgundy the indigenous red bean is simmered slowly with bacon and red wine. And throughout France roast lamb is rarely served without a *panaché,* a buttered mixture of freshly picked *haricots verts* and fresh green *flageolet* beans.

For the gardener, there are some particularly good French bean varieties to look out for:

*Beans drying in bunches for winter storing*

the previously mentioned Petit Gris, Métis and Gloire de Deuil for lovers of delicate green beans. In the mange-tout family the most prolific and certainly the tastiest variety is Princesse. Good French haricot beans include Coco, Soisson, Chevrier and Lingot.

French gardeners tend to cultivate runner beans only for their flowers, for decorative purposes, but there is a similar French variety which is good for cooking: Phénomène à Rame. It is immensely large but exquisitely tender when young, and, once podded, gives a good-flavoured haricot bean.

## *Oignon*

ONION

One of the most popular flavourings of French cuisine, and the favourite vegetable of Toulouse Lautrec, the onion has embedded itself in the kitchen garden since the Middle Ages. An ancient culinary record from Alsace shows that in those days a dish of cooked onions was served with a glass of pear schnapps in the middle of a banquet to help the digestion. It is probably for the same reason that the French today take a bowl of onion soup as a late supper after a day of gourmandizing. *Soupe à l'oignon* is often served baked in individual soup bowls with grated Gruyère cheese and a good dash of port wine.

French onion varieties include the small white Paris onion, the red from Niort – excellent for salads – and the yellow onion from Cambrai, in the North. But the most useful variety of all must be the small everlasting onion, the Rocambole – *Allium fistulosum.* The sight of this pretty lily will astonish many visitors to the kitchen garden. It never seeds but keeps producing tiny bulbs against its stems. These can be pickled or are a perfect addition to any wine sauce such as for coq-au-vin or a civet of hare or rabbit.

The *flammekueche,* one of the traditional first courses of Alsace, is a mixture of onions, tiny lardons and nutmeg spread on a thin bread dough and cooked briefly over an open fire. Another favourite of the same region is the *zeewelkueche,* or onion tart, where the onions are softened in butter, then mixed with lardons, eggs and cream.

In Picardie and most of the North, a thick sauce to accompany grilled or roast white meat is made with onions cooked until meltingly soft, while in the Basque region, onion slices are dipped in milk, then coated in flour and deep-fried in olive oil, to be served as a garnish. But the most exquisite recipe must be onions *à la bordelaise* which are stuffed with a herby mixture of chicken livers and truffles, baked in a very low oven until soft and glazed with a little nutmeg and a glass of fine champagne.

Small onions are used to flavour vinegar, gherkins and other pickles. Larger ones are bunched up and kept in a dry place throughout the winter. French onion growers will tell you that if the autumn onion has more than three layers of skin it means that winter will be harsh.

*The main ingredient of soupe à l'oignon*

## *Navet*

TURNIP

Turnip grows wild on the Breton island of Ouessant. Indigenous to Europe, this root vegetable is rich in vitamins A, B and C.

Too often associated with rich, heavy food, the small turnip is delicate in both flavour and texture. It makes a fine soup and a light purée, with a faintly smoky flavour. Baby turnips need not be peeled; their pink outer skin is a colourful addition to a dish of tender steamed young vegetables.

*Delicate in flavour, the turnip makes a light purée*

## *Oseille*

SORREL

Herb or vegetable? This is arguable. Found in most French *potagers*, sorrel can be cooked on its own or added to a dish of spinach.

It has a clean, tart taste, and its acidity combined with cream makes a fine sauce, *sauce à l'oseille,* to be served with salmon and other poached fish.

In most French homes, summer would be unimaginable without at least one sorrel soup. Mixed with potatoes, butter and cream, it is very refreshing and can be served iced in midsummer.

*Œufs à l'oseille* make a fine first course: sweat the sorrel leaves quickly in butter, spoon the purée into the base of individual ramekins, break an egg into the centre of each one, cover with a spoon of crème fraîche, season with salt and pepper and bake in a bain-marie in a medium oven (180°C / 350°F / gas mark 4) until the egg is set.

Sorrel is extremely acid and should therefore not be eaten too often.

## *Petit Pois*

PEA

The garden pea became very fashionable under the reign of Louis XIV. The French monarch was so fond of this vegetable that not only did he have it served at all royal banquets, he gave some to his courtesans to eat before bedtime, as a special treat. La Quintinie, the royal gardener, always eager to indulge the whim of His Majesty, grew peas under glass so that they could be served, freshly picked, in midwinter.

Today, mange-tout and petits pois are grown in most French gardens in spring and early summer. Among the varieties, Plein le Panier is very prolific, and the long tender Téléphone is extraordinary. The delicacy of this vegetable will only be enjoyed if it is cooked almost immediately after being picked, otherwise the sugar content turns to starch and the peas will be floury.

The main ingredient of a light summer soup, *potage St-Germain,* served with small croûtons and a touch of crème fraîche, petits pois are also served on their own as an accompaniment to fish and white meat, and often sweeten the cooking juices of braised duck or pigeon. It is said that Flaubert, who kept ducks in his yard, could not write one day for the quacking going on outside. He shouted, 'If you don't stop, I'll pod the peas!', and the whole farmyard went quiet.

In French cuisine, petits pois are rarely just boiled. Usually, they are simmered in a little water with lettuce leaves, a spring onion, a hint of savory and butter. Known as *petits pois à la française,* this recipe becomes *petits pois à la paysanne* if a few bacon lardons are added.

Peas can be dried for the winter months, when they are cooked with ham or puréed and served with grilled sausages.

## *Poireau*

LEEK

If the wild leek or *poireau des vignes* is becoming increasingly rare, the cultivated species, indispensable ingredient of many French dishes, is found in the *potager* throughout the year. Rich in vitamins A, B and C, it grows well in most soils and is resistant to frost.

Spring leeks are slender, with tender green leaves, and cook quickly. Known as pauper's asparagus since Roman times, it is served, like asparagus, with a vinaigrette sauce as a first course. It makes a handsome vegetable terrine and, when gently softened in butter, becomes the ideal accompaniment for white fish and shellfish. Tossed in butter with a few lardons, it can then be mixed with a Mornay sauce and cooked in a savoury pie crust – *tarte aux poireaux* – or used as a filling for light puff pastry – *flamishe picarde,* a dish of the North. In Normandy, where leeks grow in profusion, they are sweated in butter and then mixed with cream and sliced potatoes to be baked into a light gratin – *blanquette de poireau.*

The autumn and winter leek is large, takes a while to cook and is added to *pot-au-feu* and stews. Chopped finely, it combines with bay leaf in the concoction of *soupe au poireau.* Eaten *à la paysanne,* or puréed for a smooth finish, but always enhanced with a small knob of butter and a spoonful of crème fraîche, *soupe au poireau* is homely and comforting. Omitting butter, the same soup can be served chilled as Vichyssoise.

Among the varieties of French leeks look for Gros de Rouen; Gros du Midi; Monstrueux de Carentan, and Jaune du Poitou.

*Returning from the allotment: leeks for the soup*

*The pepper, the flavour of the Basque country*

## *Poivron*

PEPPER

Green, red, orange or yellow, the pepper belongs to the pimiento family and originated in Brazil. Explorers brought it back from the New World in the eighteenth century.

A Southern vegetable, it will only grow to full size under warm and sunny skies. The green pepper is gorged with vitamin C, and as it ripens and turns red, its vitamin A content develops too.

The brilliantly coloured, fleshy vegetable gives a fresh, perfumed flavour to salads. It is more easily digested when peeled. To do so, either blanch the pepper for a few minutes in boiling water, or roast it under the grill until the skin is black and charred all over. Place the pepper in a polythene bag and leave to cool, then peel it, cut it into fine strips and marinate for an hour or so in a dressing of fruity olive oil, lemon juice, parsley and crushed garlic, to develop the flavour. Prepared this way, peppers are delicious on their own as a first course, or can be combined with tomatoes, olives or rice in a mixed salad.

In cooking, red and green peppers are intimately associated with ratatouille – the exquisite vegetable fricassée of Provence, and they remain the vegetable mainstay of the Basque country. In the small town of Espelette, peppers festoon the south-facing sides of the houses as they dry; they will be powdered or cooked in winter dishes. Foremost among the numerous Basque recipes enhanced with the tang of peppers is *pipérade,* an omelette cooked in the oven with a *ragoût* of tomatoes and mixed peppers. *Epaule de mouton basquaise* is a delight: the shoulder of lamb is boned and stuffed with a strong herb, bread and garlic mixture before being rolled up. It is then braised in olive oil with peppers and white wine. Along the Riviera, and especially around St-Jean-de-Luz, fishermen prepare tuna fish in a *sauce basquaise* made of tomatoes, peppers and white wine. Inland, among the slopes of the Western Pyrenees, *poulet basquaise,* a chicken gently casseroled in a similar sauce, is cooked by farmers' wives.

Peppers can be preserved in vinegar, with herbs and spices, in olive oil, or between layers of sea salt to which herbs have been added. Kept in tightly sealed preserving jars, they will give a flavour of summer to *daubes* and other dishes.

## *Pomme de Terre*

POTATO

French fries, golden croquettes, aromatic *ragoûts,* silky-smooth gratins or supple purées . . . it is hard to believe that the French would have nothing to do with the miraculous tuber for such a long time. Banned in France until the late eighteenth century, the potato was described as a pernicious substance from South America which it was claimed could transmit leprosy.

It took the conviction of Antoine Parmentier, a pharmacist from the Pas-de-Calais, finally to allow the people of France to taste and grow potatoes. On 24 August 1783, Parmentier rushed to Versailles with a bunch of potato flowers for Marie-Antoinette and managed to convince Louis XVI of the many benefits of the plant. That same evening, the French king wore a potato flower as a button-hole, and the first dish of potatoes was served at the court of France.

Today, the French Agronomic Institute records over a thousand species. A valuable carbohydrate, the potato is recommended by many dieticians. Rich in vitamin C, it contains only 90 calories per 100 g / 4 oz, against rice or bread which tally 250 calories per 100 g / 4 oz. In other words, if used judiciously in cooking, with small amounts of fat, the potato is not fattening at all.

Among the garden potatoes, varieties include: Bretonne; Belle de Juillet; Saint-Malo; Charlotte; Belle de Fontenay; Saucisse (long and narrow); Ratte, and Rosa, the pink-fleshed tuber of early summer. The amazing black potato, *Solanum tuberosum,* which takes on a delicate pink colour once puréed. The winter varieties, large and floury, are ideal for soups, purées, *hachis Parmentier,* the French version of cottage pie, and gratins.

Children love this *gratin de pommes de terre.* Slice the potatoes thinly and cook gently in milk, garlic and nutmeg until just tender. Carefully lift from the pan with a slotted spoon and arrange the slices in an earthenware baking dish. Cover with crème fraîche and a generous helping of grated Emmenthal and Beaufort cheese. Bake in a hot oven (200°C / 400°F / gas mark 6) until golden-brown. Serve as a main dish with a side salad.

*Freshly gathered potatoes are washed in the stone trough outside the kitchen*

Alternatively, you may wish to prepare *pâté de pommes de terre,* a recipe from central France. The potatoes are thinly sliced and baked inside a savoury pie crust with a touch of chopped sorrel and parsley and a knob of butter. When the pie is cooked, warm cream is poured through the hole in the pastry lid, to moisten the vegetables.

In Auvergne, home of Cantal cheese, potatoes are grated, dried in a cloth and mixed with garlic and parsley. The mixture is then sautéed in butter and pounded down into a *galette,* or flat cake, as it cooks. When the underside is cooked and golden, the *galette* is turned over and cooked until crisp on the other side. Then the heat is lowered to a minimum, Cantal cheese is layered in wafer-thin slices over the surface of the *galette,* which is cooked, covered, for 15 minutes. For a main course it can also be served with ham or a thick piece of grilled bacon.

The new potato of spring and summer is firm and waxy, with yellow flesh. It stays firm as it cooks and makes good sautéed potatoes. Steamed, new potatoes are served with a herb butter. Cold new potatoes make a good salad with herrings or cold oxtail and flat parsley.

Today, in the kitchens of the *grands chefs,* the potato is elevated to the heights of gastronomy. The Ratte is steamed before being filled with the finest of butter and caviar, or is baked with a truffle, and has also been seen coupled shamelessly with fresh *foie gras* in the most outrageously extravagant potato cakes.

## *Salsifi*

SALSIFY

The agronomist Olivier de Serres introduced salsify to France as 'a root which deserves an honourable place in the kitchen garden'. Black- or white-skinned, this fine root vegetable is tender and has an intriguing, slightly smoky taste. Sown in the garden in spring, it can be dug from October onwards. Salsify flowers are attractive and decorative and it is an unusual vegetable to grow.

Buttered salsify is a good accompaniment to roast fowl. It makes a light fritter to be served on its own or as a vegetable accompaniment, with a squeeze of lemon juice. Once boiled or simmered in chicken broth, it can be baked into a silky-smooth gratin with a white or cheese sauce. In the Périgord, *tourte de poulet aux salsifis* is a light pie with a chicken, cream and salsify filling.

To prepare salsify, first scrape off the skin, wearing gloves to protect your hands from staining. Rinse the root in water with lemon juice added, to help keep its fine ivory colour while cooking.

## *Tomate*

TOMATO

The taste of sun-gorged, garden-grown tomato is irreplaceable. The firm, freshly picked fruit, cut into thick slices or quarters and tossed with chopped chives or spring onions in a fruity olive oil, with lemon juice, salt and pepper, must be the simplest yet most satisfying first course of summer. Allow yourself the exquisite pleasure of dipping crusty bread in the vinaigrette moistened with the pink juices of the tomato – the taste has no equal.

And yet, as with the potato, it took a lot of convincing to persuade the French to eat the fruit of the *poumo d'amour* – the love apple – as the people of Provence first called it. Two centuries ago, it was grown only as a decorative plant. Today, any keen gardener keeps at least two or three varieties in his garden.

*The dramatic colours of summer's yield*

In cooking, the tomato was first used in a sauce. French gastronome Brillat-Savarin declared the sauce worthy of almost any meat. It has certainly been proved so in Provence. From Monte Carlo to Collioure, *sauce provençale* is used hot or cold to complement grilled meat, fish and egg dishes.

The cooks of Provence make splendid tomato soups, adding fine pasta, a few haricot beans or even a few grains of rice. And if today the *tomate farçie* – stuffed tomato – can be found throughout France, there are still some especially good tomato recipes indigenous to the South of France.

The best-known and most copied of all must be the *tomate provençale,* which rivals *pommes d'amour grillées*: tomatoes are halved and seasoned with crushed garlic, parsley, thyme and a hint of fennel; they are then grilled and served with a knob of anchovy butter on top.

Stuffed *à l'antiboise,* the tomatoes are hollowed out and filled with a mixture of anchovies chopped with tuna fish, black and green olives, thyme, parsley and garlic. Olive oil is poured over and the tomatoes are baked in a very hot oven (225°C / 425°F / gas mark 8) for a few minutes.

Near Valréas, I was given a delicate potato and tomato *tian*, or gratin. First, onions are sliced and sautéed in olive oil, then layered with tomatoes and potatoes. Grated cheese and wild thyme is sprinkled on each layer and you must finish with a layer of tomatoes. The dish is then baked in a hot oven (200°C / 400°F / gas mark 6) for 45 minutes or until the potatoes are cooked.

But the best dish of all was the *tatin de tomates* – an upsidedown tomato tart – which I shared with keen gardeners in the hills of the Ventoux.

In full sun the tomato plant produces fruit from July until October. The main French varieties include: Cerise; Poire; Olive; Reine des Hâtives; Sans Pareille; Pierrette, and Grosse Marmande – the ridged species which can weight pounds and has hardly any seeds.

Tomatoes for salads are a subject in themselves and can be found in the French Salad Garden on page 37.

## The Salad Garden

Eaten in France since the Middle Ages, salad leaves, whichever the species, must be the choicest vegetable of the kitchen garden. Any lettuce, just picked, thoroughly washed and immediately tossed in a vinaigrette dressing, is sweet, crunchy and refreshing.

In most French homes *la salade* remains a separate course at luncheon and dinner, served on its own for digestive purposes. In some regions it is served with cheese and a seasoning of chopped shallots.

Apart from *mesclun,* a mixture of salad leaves served in the South of France, any green salad with the addition of another vegetable such as peppers, tomatoes or cucumbers, is called *salade composée. Salade composée* is served as a first course, cold or lukewarm, when piping-hot lardons of bacon or chicken livers fried in a little olive oil with herbs are added.

Both Ronsard and Rabelais praised the delicacy of salad, and the gastronome Brillat-Savarin described it as 'refreshing without enfeebling, and comforting without irritating'.

### *Chicorée et Endive*

CHICORY AND ENDIVE

A wild plant from Egypt, chicory was introduced to France in the fifteenth century. The four main cultivated varieties are the sweet and firm *scarole,* which is usually served on its own with a chervil or parsley dressing. Next is the slightly bitter *frisée.* The blanched centre, which is quite mild, is served with mashed hard-boiled eggs and a chive dressing or with lukewarm accompaniments such as sautéed potatoes and lardons, or chicken livers lightly sautéed in butter with garlic and a dash of lemon juice or port. *Frisée* is also excellent with a fruity olive oil dressing served with a dish of thinly sliced pan-fried wild mushrooms.

The other two varieties are grown only by the expert gardener, for they require a lot of attention and intensive blanching. One, *endive,* is the winter salad of France, originally grown in the North; new hybrids are easier to grow in the domestic garden. It needs to be dressed with a strong mustardy dressing if served on its own or is excellent with a walnut oil and balsamic vinegar dressing with beetroot, cold poultry, a few walnuts and onion rings. It is a must as a base for salads of warm langoustine or coquille St Jacques and is the French Northern accompaniment to *potjeveleish,* a dish of potted veal.

The last variety, *barbe de capucin,* is only for the attuned palate. It resembles a long dandelion and is very bitter even when blanched.

### *Laitue*

LETTUCE

More than 100 varieties may be found in the French garden. Among them, the most common is the soft lettuce which can be so sweet if picked young from the garden. Usually the hearts are eaten raw whilst the outer leaves are sweated with butter to cook peas. *Romaine* or Webb lettuce is crunchier, a good summer salad. Heart and outer leaves are equally tender. It is good with a mild dressing and plenty of freshly chopped shallot and a hint of garlic. Once tossed, it can be sprinkled with chopped chervil or chives.

A newish fine variety is the *feuille de chêne* or oak-leaf lettuce. It has a natural nutty taste which can be enhanced by a dressing made with a touch of walnut oil and sherry vinegar.

*A medley of lettuces*

## *Mâche*

LAMBS LETTUCE

This is probably the finest of all salad leaves. The regional French names describe its soft consistency and sweet taste: *doucette, boursette, galinette, blanchette.* It has a long, thin, velvety leaf and is delicious mixed with cooked beetroot and walnut kernels.

## *Mesclun*

MIXED SALAD LEAVES

A mixture of cultivated and wild salad leaves, mainly eaten in Provence. Among these are chickweed, salad rocket, orach – purple and green – nasturtium leaves and summer purslane. The mixed flavours are interesting and delicate and the dressing should not be too overpowering. A light vinaigrette is ideal.

Recently the French have re-adopted a tradition popular in the fourteenth and fifteenth centuries of decorating their green salads with edible flowers, such as nasturtium, borage, chives and meadow crane's bill.

## *Radis*

RADISH

It would be difficult not to include in the salad garden the radish, young and tender hors-d'œuvre of spring, traditionally served simply with salt and bread and butter.

More popular are the small round or long pink variety, or the large red summer radish – *rave* – which has a stronger tang and should be eaten with plenty of bread and butter or sliced in a *salade composée.*

## *Tomate*

TOMATO

Finally, one must mention the salad tomato hybrids. Small, firm and almost seedless, they include: Beauté Blanche, a small, ridged, pure white tomato; Polonaise, a bright orange cherry tomato; Jaune, another cherry tomato, but bright yellow; Poire Jaune and Poire Rouge, both minute and pear-shaped. Finally, the most exquisite of all, the Groseille Jaune et Rouge: fleshy and very juicy, this looks just like a redcurrant.

*On the garden bench: a summer gathering*

*Pickled cherry tomatoes, a useful addition to summer salads*

## The Herb Garden

*'Volumus quod in horti omnes herbas habeant'. Charlemagne, King of France and Emperor of the Occident*

*(Eighth century AD)*

In addition to their medicinal qualities, herbs give flavour to the blandest of dishes and an attractive finishing touch as garnishes for serving platters. The mere mention of their names evokes limpid blue skies, sun-drenched landscapes and the unmistakable aroma of Mediterranean dishes.

For it is on Mediterranean soil that the cultivation of herbs began, in the mists of time. The ancient Egyptians flavoured their beer with mint and oregano; the Greeks added cumin and coriander seeds to their bread; and myriad herbs and spices complemented the soups, meat dishes and stews served at Roman banquets. In the first century AD, the Roman epicure Apicius served broccoli seasoned with mint, rue, coriander, young cabbage shoots, oil and wine.

Later on, in the Middle Ages, knights brought back more exotica from the Crusades. Rich spices were used almost to excess, turning marinades into heady perfume and masking all original tastes, until cooks with more tutored palates eventually created the discerning and subtle art of cooking with herbs.

*Coriander: a pungent herb used since the dawn of time*

In France, the monks first perpetuated the ancient traditions of cultivating herbs in the secret gardens of their monasteries. They introduced us to herb teas, sweet liqueurs and infusions. By the end of the sixteenth century, with the cultivation of vegetables becoming fashionable amongst royalty and high society, the herb garden crowned the intricacy of the landscaped kitchen garden.

Today in France, not even the smallest garden, terrace or window-box is without its clump of parsley, chives or thyme. Could one imagine a summer in the South without the intoxicating fragrance of basil? Whether it is chives for a simple omelette, a few stems of freshly picked parsley to enhance the flavour of French beans, or some potent combination for an elaborate dish, the gathering of aromatic foliage or spicy seeds remains the rewarding pleasure of the inventive cook, professional or amateur.

### *Angélique*

ANGELICA

A tall, lush plant with highly aromatic stems and leaves, in France angelica is also known as the herb of the Holy Spirit. It grows wild in the mountainous regions of the Pyrenees and the Alps. It is one of the ingredients of Chartreuse, the smooth green and amber liqueur brewed by monks for its medicinal purposes and drunk by all for its wonderfully soothing after-effects. In the Poitou, near Niort, freshly candied angelica is used in soufflés and pastries. The stems, macerated with *eau-de-vie*, make a good home-made liqueur. The fresh leaves give a delicate flavour to *compote* and fruit *coulis*.

Stems and leaves should be gathered before the plant starts flowering.

Herb-flavoured oils

## *Basilic*

BASIL

A sun-lover, this plant of Indian origin was introduced to France from Italy. Long-leaved basil preserved in oil is a good condiment, and purple basil brings colour and flavour to summer salads, but it is sweet basil that is to be found in most gardens. A delicate plant, it is grown mainly in pots, in full sun, and can be brought indoors to thrive on a sunny window-sill throughout the winter months and early spring.

Basil's inimitable aroma brings sunshine to tomato salads and egg dishes. Pounded with garlic, oil and cheese into a paste – *pistou* – it perfumes fresh beans and tomato soups as well as gratins and pasta. Mixed with butter, a touch of olive oil and freshly ground black pepper, it gives steamed new potatoes an unrivalled taste. With its antiseptic qualities, basil is excellent for the digestion and helps prevent food poisoning.

Leaves should be gathered just before use and torn rather than chopped for the full flavour.

## *Cerfeuil*

CHERVIL

The fine, jagged leaves have a slight tang of aniseed; the young shoots have a stronger flavour than the larger leaves. Chervil is to be found in every French herb garden, next to parsley.

It particularly suits green salad dressings. Try a Kos or Webb lettuce with a vinaigrette dressing made with chopped chervil leaves and a mashed hard-boiled egg.

Chervil stimulates the digestion and is good sprinkled over heavier dishes such as casseroles or fricassées. It also makes a fine soup which is worth considering as part of a summer menu.

Gather the stems just before use and tear up the young leaves rather than chopping them.

## *Ciboulette*

CHIVES

Also known in France as *civette*, or even *fines herbes*, this allium, cousin of the onion, grows in small clumps, with fine pink flowers in the summer. Its use is widespread in French cuisine where the *omelette aux fines herbes* is always a good stand-by for last-minute guests or a quickly prepared dinner.

The chopped leaves are sprinkled over salads and give a more delicate flavour than a whole chopped onion to any salad dressing. In summer, the pink flowers, which are edible, can also be used to garnish salads.

Chives are one of the main ingredients of piquant *sauce gribiche,* and is excellent spooned into cottage cheese or fromage blanc with freshly ground sea salt and pepper.

Chives thrive in pots as well as in the garden and should be cut regularly to help regrowth. Cut leaves, leaving 5 cm / 2 in regrowth. Chop finely on a chopping board, using a sharp knife.

## *Estragon*

TARRAGON

Of Asian origin, tarragon entered the gardens and kitchens of France in the sixteenth century, where it has been popular ever since.

With the subtle and stunning aroma of its fine long leaves, tarragon has remained the great classic of French cuisine, despite the use of more fashionable herbs over the years. *Béarnaise, ravigote, gribiche, tartare, mayonnaise* . . . the perfume of tarragon is found in all these sauces. It mixes rapturously with cream and butter to complement seafood, fish and chicken, as well as potatoes and crisp young vegetables. *Poulet à l'estragon* will always be a French classic. Bottled in a good vinegar, tarragon adds piquancy to salads and sauces throughout the year.

*Herbs for sale in a Brittany market*

## *Géranium Odorant*

SCENTED GERANIUM

No fewer than twenty-two species of the scented pelargonium may be found at the Bureau et Fils nursery in Savennières on the bank of the river Loire. The sweet-scented pelargonium is a useful and very decorative addition to any herb garden. Rose-scented, lemon-scented, peppery or orange-scented, to name only a few varieties, the leaves can be infused to flavour sauces, jams and butter. The pervasive aroma of a leaf placed on the base of a cake tin will give the simplest of sponge cakes an unforgettable flavour.

Geranium is good with tomatoes, potatoes and poached fruit. The inventive cook may well keep the secrets of unusual flavour combinations.

Among the varieties recommended for cooking are: Prince of Orange; Prince Ruppert; Radula; Robert's Lemon Rose; Tomentosum; Endsleigh; Crispum, and Vitifolium.

## *Laurier*

BAY

The main ingredient of bouquet garni, bay is so widely used in French cuisine that no garden should be without its bay tree. The fresh leaves, torn in half, will exude an aroma which is indispensable to marinades, *court-bouillon* and broths, as well as many pâtés and terrines.

The bay tree, which can grow as high as 4 m / 12 ft, loves sun and heat, but will thrive in northern climates if well exposed.

5F

## *Marjolaine*

MARJORAM

The cultivated cousin of oregano, an ancient culinary herb supposedly created by Venus, the goddess of love, marjoram was introduced to France in the Middle Ages.

In cooking, marjoram is good with grilled meat and chicken, mixed with other herbs in an omelette or added to baked vegetables. Sprinkle it on onion or tomato tarts and bring a holiday aroma to your kitchen. Use marjoram sparingly, however, for it has a strong flavour.

The fine leaves should be gathered before the plant bursts into a multitude of small pink and white flowers, which are then best left to the bees. A melliferous plant, marjoram can also be used as a natural dye.

## *Persil*

PARSLEY

The most widespread of all herbs, parsley is rich in vitamin C. When chewed raw, it is a useful palliative to the after-fumes of alcohol, and it also clears the mouth after eating garlic.

The two varieties, flat-leaved or curly, can be used to equal effect in cooking. It is therefore recommended to grow both permanently in the herb garden as the parsley is indispensable to so many forms of cooking: in bouquet garni, sauces, marinades, as a garnish, and so on. Parsley also makes a fine soup when combined with potatoes and onions. Try frying curly parsley quickly in oil or butter and serve it as a vegetable with fish. When chopped very finely, and mixed with garlic, it then becomes *persillade,* which is a useful last-minute addition to many dishes,whether baked, grilled or fried.

## *Romarin*

ROSEMARY

Highly aromatic, rosemary grows wild on Mediterranean soil. With its small orchid-like blue flowers in summer, it is an attractive plant to grow in the kitchen garden. Its essence helps the digestion but it needs to be used judiciously as the flavour can be overpowering. Add a small stem to the cooking of less digestible dried vegetables such as chick-peas, haricot beans or lentils.

One of the ingredients of the Southern bouquet garni, rosemary is a good bactericide and is recommended for the marinade of meat in the summer as well as game in autumn and winter.

Rosemary with roast or grilled lamb is no secret, but try it with olive oil on roasted or grilled chicken. It gives the meat an unparalleled taste.

## *Sarriette*

SAVORY

The smell of savory evokes Provence and balmy undergrowths. Because of its peppery taste, it is the *pebre d'ase*, the 'donkey's pepper' of Provence where it is used as a condiment with goat's cheese. Planted in a protected position, the small shrub with its dense stems and tiny curly leaves will thrive in almost any garden.

Savory gives a magic flavour to broad beans and fresh haricot beans and is excellent with duck, calves' liver and white fish. A combination of fresh figs, goat's cheese and savory makes a succulent, semi-sweet dessert.

## *Sauge*

SAGE

Bruise a leaf of this soft green plant and you can smell the heady, lemony aroma. The Latin name, *salvia,* comes from *salvere,* to save. Throughout history, sage has been regarded as a powerful healing plant, said to be capable of prolonging life. For this reason it was grown in abundance in all the royal gardens of France.

Sage is an attractive plant to grow in the herb garden. In cooking, with its pronounced flavour, it needs to be used on its own, or maybe just with thyme. A chicken fricassée with butter, sage leaves, a touch of thyme and white wine, but no garlic or onion, is a delight.

Try macerating sage leaves in melted butter for a few minutes, then use the butter to dress boiled or steamed potatoes. Sage leaves make excellent fritters to be served crisp and piping hot with summer drinks.

Also, an infusion of sage leaves in the cooking water gives a delicate flavour to steamed chicken or young vegetables.

## *Thym*

THYME

Indigenous to Europe, the wild carpeting of Southern soils, thyme has always been recognized for its medicinal qualities, along with its delicate essence, thymol.

With its antiseptic and digestive qualities, it also helps to fix the iron which is found in food. From lemon to verbena, according to the species, its evocative tang floats in the stocks and sauces of all French classic dishes such as *daube*, *pot-au-feu*, soups and terrines.

Could one conceive of a bouquet garni without a stem of thyme? Bottled in olive oil, it will flavour marinades and grilled meat. Try macerating olives with thyme, olive oil and garlic. Mix thyme-flavoured olive oil with capers to accompany smoked salmon.

# The French Fruit Garden

Summer in the fruit garden offers the extreme delight of satisfying both hunger and thirst, the tactile pleasure of picking or choosing the ripest fruit, and the sensuous gratification of biting into soft, juicy flesh gorged with sun and health.

There is also the anticipation of convivial desserts, old and new recipes. Summer gives us the opportunity to reminisce over the tart Grand'-mère always made with the first redcurrants, and remember the plums and apricots she used to dry in the sun for winter puddings. At the same time, it gives us the chance to enthuse over such recipes as the mixed plum charlotte that Tante Claire invented last year.

And suddenly, one midsummer day, when the yield has turned to glut, it is bottling and jam-making time, and the whole house is filled with the sweet perfume of fruit being poached or boiled in copper pans. Vari-coloured nectars will be left to set in small glass jars or will be mixed with *eau-de-vie* for winter liqueurs.

Then comes September and autumnal fruitfulness. Grapes are delicately picked with scissors, little bags are placed around pears to protect them from the wasps, and as the first mist of wintry mornings lies upon the orchard, the precious last apples of the year are wrapped in tissue paper and laid on wooden shelves in the attic to await the culinary celebration of Christmas.

*Summer in a Provençal fruit garden*

## Red Fruit

### Cassis

BLACKCURRANT

The blackcurrant was first grown in the region of Cassis, near Toulon, in the sixteenth century. Once the ever popular recipe for *liqueur de cassis* was invented in the mid-nineteenth century, it was and is still mass-produced in Burgundy, especially around Dijon.

The liqueur recipe is no secret and blackcurrant bushes are a feature of most French gardens. The firm and juicy berries are delicious mixed with redcurrants and soft brown sugar as a summer fruit salad. Prepared at least one hour in advance, the mixture exudes an exquisite juice which is excellent served with yoghurt or fromage frais.

Blackcurrant jam and jelly are prepared in the French households mainly to be eaten with brioche, a buttery speciality loaf to which they are the perfect accompaniment.

Kept in *eau-de-vie*, or an oak-aged wine vinegar, blackcurrant is good added to braised duck or *magret de canard* about 5 minutes before the end of cooking time.

One of the richest fruits in vitamin C, blackcurrant is reputed to be good for the eyesight.

### Cerise

CHERRY

The wild cherry tree is the precursor of all spring fruit blossom. In France, the first cultivated cherry trees appeared in the Middle Ages around the town of Montmorency in the Val d'Oise, near Paris, where Jean-Jacques Rousseau found the bucolic retreat he longed for.

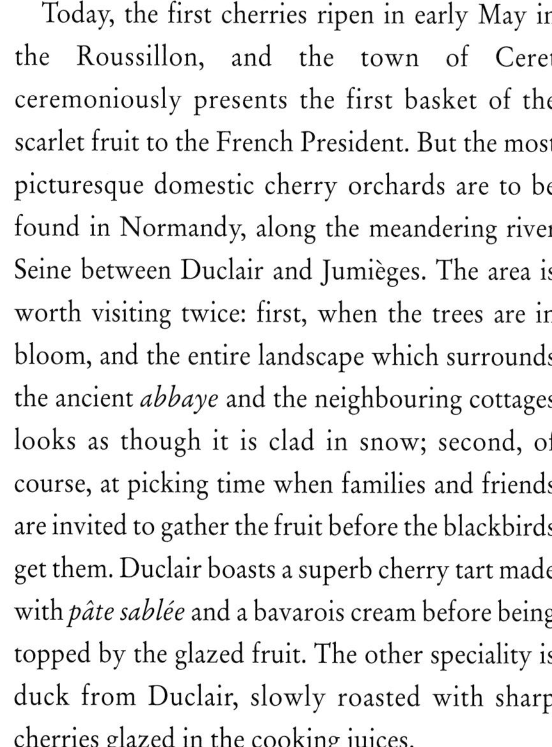

Today, the first cherries ripen in early May in the Roussillon, and the town of Ceret ceremoniously presents the first basket of the scarlet fruit to the French President. But the most picturesque domestic cherry orchards are to be found in Normandy, along the meandering river Seine between Duclair and Jumièges. The area is worth visiting twice: first, when the trees are in bloom, and the entire landscape which surrounds the ancient *abbaye* and the neighbouring cottages looks as though it is clad in snow; second, of course, at picking time when families and friends are invited to gather the fruit before the blackbirds get them. Duclair boasts a superb cherry tart made with *pâte sablée* and a bavarois cream before being topped by the glazed fruit. The other speciality is duck from Duclair, slowly roasted with sharp cherries glazed in the cooking juices.

In all, there are around 500 varieties of cherries in France. Not surprisingly, recipes abound. In *cerises à l'eau-de-vie* whole cherries are left to macerate in a good fruit schnapps, with sugar, for at least three months, sealed in special jars. They are then delicately, almost ceremoniously, spooned by grandmothers or elderly aunts into special little blue or pink glasses after lunch or dinner. It is always a pleasure to share this ritualistic offering.

Another recipe is *soupe de cerises,* which was originally served with bread as a warm first course in the Savoie region. It is now served ice-cold as a dessert, either with home-made tuile biscuits or to accompany a creamy rice pudding. The cherries are cooked for 10 minutes in a good claret with a stick of cinnamon and the grated rind of a lemon. The juice is then reduced and thickened with a spoonful of redcurrant jelly and left to cool for a few hours before serving.

Preserved in vinegar, with allspice and fresh tarragon, cherries are an excellent and original condiment to serve with cold turkey or ham. It is best to choose Morello cherries for this recipe.

Look for: Cerise de Montmorency; Coeur de Pigeon; Bigarreau Napoléon; Reine Hortense, and Impératrice Eugénie.

## *Fraise*

STRAWBERRY

The original strawberry is the highly fragrant alpine strawberry known in France as *fraise des bois.* It is from this species that the cultivation of the garden strawberry began, as early as the Middle Ages.

Gastronomic customs, like fashion, are often revived. It is said that in the eighteenth century, the ladies of French high society met in the afternoon to eat succulent strawberries dipped in sugar and thick cream.

If the strawberry has inspired agronomists and gardeners, it has also inspired artists, the best-known painting of the fruit being *Le Panier de Fraises des Bois*, by Chardin (1731).

Strawberries have of course been a constant inspiration to the cook. *Tarte aux fraises*, with or without *crème pâtissiere*, *millefeuille*, jams and other specialities such as *fraisier*, a light cake, make a regular appearance on summer menus in most French homes.

*Jam-making in the Loire valley*

## *Framboise*

RASPBERRY

The original wild raspberry was white. A beautiful legend recounts that Ida, daughter of the King of Crète, wanting to calm the cries of the young Zeus, bent down to pick him a white raspberry, and as her breast caught one of the thorns of the plant, a drop of the nymph's blood fell upon the fruit. The raspberry has stayed a rich pink colour ever since.

Red raspberries grow wild in France, in the Alps and on the slopes of the Massif Central. But the cultivated varieties, which are the most delicate, grow throughout the country, especially in Alsace where raspberries are used to make an excellent white schnapps. A *liqueur de framboise,* also known as *ratafia*, is prepared by most French housewives, together with fine tartlets, raspberry jelly, sorbets, ice-cream and feather-light cold soufflés.

Among the French species, look for: Belle de Fontenay; Merveille des Quatre Saisons; Framboise de Homet; Sucrée de Metz, and Surprise de Metz.

## *Groseille*

REDCURRANT

An indigenous fruit of Normandy where it still abounds in most gardens, the berries are either red or white. They can be macerated in sugar for 1–2 hours and served as a refreshing summer dessert, or are delicious spooned into the cavity of halved Charentais or Cavaillon melons. The redcurrant is mostly used for the making of jelly which in Normandy is traditionally served for Sunday afternoon tea with *gâche*, a kind of yeasty brioche, and a caramelized cold and creamy rice pudding. Topped with a light meringue, redcurrants also make an exquisite tart.

A related variety is *groseille à maquereau,* the gooseberry. It is served, once again in Normandy, puréed with grilled mackerel – hence the name. It also makes a good *compote* to be served with crème fraîche or fromage blanc.

## *Rhubarbe*

RHUBARB

Originally Chinese, rhubarb was introduced to Europe, via the British Isles, in the eighteenth century. This attractive garden plant was first grown by monks for its medicinal virtues until the excellence of the stalks was discovered in cookery. *Compote,* jams and meringued tarts, as well as light and refreshing hot soufflés, are made in France in the summer months.

In fact rhubarb is a leguminous plant rather than a fruit and is also excellent braised with goose, duck or pork. It melts in the sauce and gives a secret tang to the dish. In *nouvelle cuisine* it has been introduced, with cream, as a sauce for salmon and white fish.

*Gathering of flowers and rhubarb in the spring garden*

*Sun-gorged rhubarb jam*

## Fruit with Stones

### Abricot

APRICOT

Introduced to Europe in the fifteenth century from Armenia, this fruit, which is rich in carotene and vitamin C, needs plenty of sun and warmth and is mostly found in the Southern French garden. To be savoured at its best, raw, it must be very ripe and almost ready to fall off the tree. The outside is a rich reddish-orange and the flesh inside, the colour of a nectar.

Like most good ripe fruit, it is almost a shame to cook it. But the French are fond of apricot jam, often served at breakfast with crispy bread or hot croissants. Apricot sauce or *coulis* is made to accompany blander stewed fruit.

French apricot tart is made with feather light puff pastry spread with a layer of *crème pâtissiere* and topped with glazed apricots. But in recent years, inspired by the original *tarte Tatin* made with apples, the recipe for succulent *Tatin d'abricots* is slowly appearing on French tables.

French varieties include: Gros Rouge de Rivesaltes; Bergeron de Provence, and the small Petit Bulida.

*Gathering ripeness from the orchard*

## *Pêche*

PEACH

Originating from Persia, the white peach was also indigenous to China. The first French peaches were white and are making a comeback with the keen gardener who recognizes its extremely fine taste. Often a small fruit, it will grow in Northern climates if planted in a sunny spot protected from the wind.

The French Southern hybrids include the yellow large peach – *pêche abricot* – and the *brugnon* or nectarine which has not got the velvety skin of the peach but a more fragrant taste.

Peaches can be grown along walls on an espalier. This mode of culture was in fact devised by the royal gardener, La Quintinie, who planted numerous varieties at Versailles, such as Belle de Chevreuse and Belle de Vitry, as well as Belle de Montreuil. Today, peaches are grown in most well-exposed gardens, but it is in Provence and the South-West that they reach full ripeness and taste.

Too many ancient recipes have impaired the excellence of this fruit. They included fritters, heavy mixtures with rice, macerations in kirsch. The best recipe is probably the one created for Madame de Récamier, for whom peaches were simply poached in their own juice and served cold with single cream. The chefs of *nouvelle cuisine* have made interesting peach terrines, complementing the flavour of the fruit with its own *coulis* or adding a small quantity of raspberries.

There are more than 100 varieties of peaches in France today. Among the best, let us mention old varieties such as Amsdem; Précoce de Croncels; Précoce de Felignies; Précoce de Hale; Reine des Vergers, and Téton de Vénus.

It would be a shame not to mention the exquisite *pêche de vigne*. Grown mostly among the vines of Burgundy, it is a small fruit with a deep purple, velvety skin and a deep purple flesh which has a taste and consistency all its own. Peeled and soaked in a good red wine and brown sugar for an hour, it is a delight.

## *Prune*

PLUM

The very first plum was brought back to France by the Crusaders from Damas.

The mere mention of this fruit immediately evokes the South-West where the plums from Agen are dried in the sun to be soaked in Armagnac, filled with rich almond paste for Christmas or used in the sauces of rich hare civets or fricassées of goose, duck and turkey.

In Nantes, in the Loire Valley, a *matelote* of river fish is concocted with a rich Burgundy wine, sage, small onions and prunes. In the same region, loin of pork is stuffed with prunes and slowly baked in a covered earthenware dish. In summer, the Sunday ritualistic dessert of the same region is *pâté de prunes,* a pie made with *pâte brisée* and filled with Reine-Claude plums, named after the wife of King François I.

Finally, plums evoke Alsace and hot *quetschelkueche* tarts, made with the fragrant, indigenous purple Quetsche plum and baked on a fine *pâte brisée,* then dusted with cinnamon and icing sugar. *Clafoutis* are made with the tiny Mirabelle, a yellow plum speckled with red, so fragrant that it is also used to make a fine schnapps. In Alsace, plum jam is served with hot *kugelhopf* for breakfast: Quetsche are turned into light mousses to fill meringue Vacherin together with home-made almond ice-cream. When caramelized in brown sugar and butter it is then mixed with red cabbage to accompany roast goose or venison.

*The bloom of the plums seen against the antique wickerwork*

Among French plum varieties look for Reine-Claude, the honeyed greengage; Mirabelle, which needs to be eaten almost over-ripe to exude its full perfume; Damas de Tours and Perdrigon and, of course, the excellent Quetsche which also makes good *compotes* to be served with fromage frais, yoghurt or walnut bread.

## Fruit with Pips

### *Coing*

QUINCE

An ancient, gnarled quince tree is a handsome sight against a south-facing garden wall or even the front of any old house. The spring blossom is a delicate pink and extremely decorative, and the pear-shaped fruit is good in jellies, or mixed with apples in a tart or *compote*. The taste is tart but flavoursome, and in the region of Orleans quince is cooked into a fruit paste – *cotignac* – which is served as a sweetmeat for Christmas.

The French varieties include: the highly perfumed Cognassier du Portugal; the juicy Champion, and the Monstrueux de Vranga which bears huge fruit.

### *Figue*

FIG

The ripe purple fruit with the bloom still on its skin is a beautiful sight. When cut open, the taste is as if a honey-bee had made love to the sun. A freshly picked ripe fig for breakfast is one of the hedonistic pleasures of life. Baked in a small tartlet with a cream made of pistachios and mild yoghurt, it becomes rapture.

The fig tree, which came from the gardens of Babylon, first appeared in France in Argenteuil, near Paris, in the fourteenth century, and was then grown intensively by La Quintinie in the royal gardens of Versailles. The fig will ripen in any protected sunny spot but reaches best maturity in the Mediterranean climate. Red, black, white, yellow, round or ovoid, the fruit is always succulent. A rich source of vitamins A, B and C, it is very nourishing. Raw, it can be served with raw smoked ham as a first course, and is good with any ewe's milk cheese from the Pyrenees or *coeur à la crème*, heart-shaped cottage cheese, as well as fresh goat's cheese.

Figs are an unusual addition to a fricassée of veal or pork, make excellent *compotes* and are exquisite caramelized in baking foil over an open fire.

Among the French varieties look for: Figue de Marseille; Verte des Dames; Violette de Solliès; Barnisotte Noire; Verte Brune; Servantine, and Figue de Bordeaux.

*Figs, the fruit of the Mediterranean climate*

## *Poire*

PEAR

*An afternoon collation in Normandy: pears and buttered bread*

The pear was first cultivated by the Romans who introduced it to Europe. In the Middle Ages twelve varieties were known in France; today the list of species reaches roughly 1600. The oldest pear is Bon Chrétien, a rare variety these days and highly prized by those who are still lucky enough to have a tree in their orchard. French pears are classified by the quality of their flesh, which is variously described as buttery, brittle, melting in the mouth, but, above all, by their stage of maturity: the fruit will ripen, according to variety, from June to the end of November.

The first pear of the year is the Petite de la Saint Jean, small, very juicy and full of flavour. It is followed in July by the Doyenne de Juillet, another small fruit, and the Guyot, a large, yellow fruit. The flesh is fine and it is excellent for cooking. There would not be an August, of course, without the William's yellow or red. This pear is exceptionally juicy and flavoursome, and should be eaten when very ripe.

In September, the Beurré Hardy matures and is excellent for tarts and charlottes as well as jam. Also look for the Louise-Bonne. This small pear originates from the Cotentin Peninsula and is ideal baked with red wine and spices.

Finally, we get to the species which, if stored carefully, will keep throughout the winter. Among them: Doyenné du Comice; Duchesse d'Angoulême; Crassane and Passe-Crassane, both large green pears, which will keep until April.

When driving through France it is interesting to notice that pear trees grow along the front of most vicarages. The two species most widely grown in this position are Poire du Curé and Bon Chrétien. There is nothing particularly holy about the species but they derive from an old French tradition of bartering fruit and vegetables. The countryman brought apples to the curate, who, in exchange, shared his crop of pears.

Some autumn species are called *poires à couteau.* They will ripen sufficiently to be eaten raw, as a fruit. But what an exquisite taste they have when wrapped in a thin layer of puff pastry and baked in the oven until the pastry has puffed up and the natural sugar of the fruit has caramelized inside. Served hot from the oven they are called *douillon, bourdelot* or *rabotte,* according to the region.

In Normandy, another tiny pear is grown mainly to make *poiré*, a pear champagne also known as *cidre de poire*. It is a refreshing drink with a low alcohol content and can also be used in cooking: added to the cooking juices of a guinea-fowl or roast pork, it gives the gravy an unusual tang.

In central France pears are used for *clafoutis*: they are first slightly caramelized in butter, then baked in a sweet batter in the oven. The *poirat* is a pie in which thinly sliced pears are baked, with warm cream poured through a hole in the centre of the pastry lid to moisten the fruit just before serving. Like apple tarts, pear tarts can consist of a simple layer of thinly sliced fruit over a thin *pâte brisée,* which is known as *tarte fine aux poires.* Pears baked inside a pie crust with a cream and almond mixture become *tarte normande* or *bourdaloue*.

This summer, I was served an interesting main course of caramelized roast pork served with pears baked in a savoury béchamel sauce as an accompaniment. The pears, which were firm, gave an exotic taste to the roast meat, especially once the caramel of the meat gravy blended with the béchamel.

*Early windfalls in the apple orchard*

## Pomme

APPLE

As the biblical legend of this fruit does not apply either to gardening or cookery, let us simply note that a monk and poet, Raoul Tortaire, drank a pitcher of cider in an inn near Bayeux in the eleventh century. Which means that by then the apple must have already been quite firmly established in Normandy.

In the Middle Ages, apples were used a great deal in cooking and there is record of a soup served in the Loire Valley made with apple cubes, chicken broth, saffron, spices and butter. Today, the apple is still the fruit most used in savoury as well as sweet cooking. Sautéed in butter with salt and pepper, it accompanies white meat, black pudding and fresh *foie gras.* In Southern Normandy, little quails are placed in the centre of large cooking apples which are then wrapped in puff pastry and slowly baked in the oven. Pheasants are casseroled with apples, and slices of apple soaked in Calvados are even added to rabbit or game terrines.

As a dessert, apple is the most popular fruit for tarts, and an ideal filling for pancakes and sweet omelettes. It also makes soufflés, fritters, and charlottes with buttered stale bread. Baked with butter in a hot oven it is still probably the most popular of homely desserts.

This book deals with the indigenous varieties of France and Europe, so I will ban any mention of Golden Delicious, Starking, Richared and Granny Smith and favour the old species which, thanks to the efforts of passionate gardeners, are not only still around but making a real comeback for their individual flavour. Among them: Reinette Grise; Calville, the Christmas apple of yesteryear; the tiny red Api; Reinette du Mans; Reine des Reinettes; Clochard, and the Belle de Boskoop, so good in tarts and *compotes.*

*The gift of Dionysius by Mont Ventoux*

## *Raisin*

GRAPE

The gift of Dionysius, grapes are mostly associated with the making of wine, but good indigenous *raisins de table* – dessert grapes – grow well in France from the Loire Valley to all the Mediterranean regions, as well as Burgundy.

King François I had the first Chasselas – supposedly the finest of grapes – planted in 1530 at Thomery, near Fontainebleau. To this day, the grapes are picked at their right point of ripeness and each bunch is kept with its stem in a small vase of water in the cellar. That way, grapes will be served fresh until December. Most domestic grape growers use this preserving process – a far cry from the industrial laser methods.

In cooking, grapes make a fine jelly, light tartlets made with *pâte sablée* and topping for a sweet custard. White grapes are traditionally added 15 minutes before the end of cooking time to roast quail – *caille à la vigneronne* – and black grapes are equally used, often with a few slices of cooking apples as well, with partridge or pheasant. Kept in spiced vinegar, mixed white and black grapes make an excellent condiment for white meat and especially cold turkey.

Among good French table grapes look for: Chasselas Doré de Fontainebleau; Napoléon, a firm, large black grape; the black Gamay; and finally Muscat Blanc, and Muscat Noir de Hambourg which bites back like a good glass of Beaume de Venise or a fine Gewürztraminer.

# Citrus Fruit

## *Citron*

LEMON

Only introduced to France in the Middle Ages, it was used then for its therapeutic and medicinal virtues. Today it is the constant companion of any fish dish, is good with oysters and makes a fine tart: in contrast with the deep English lemon meringue pie, the French version is wafer-thin. In Provence it is made with a *pâte sablée* flavoured with a little lemon rind, and the filling is simply a mixture of 2 eggs and 1 egg yolk with the juice of 2 large lemons, 100 g / 4 oz caster sugar and 100 g / 4 oz melted unsalted butter. Baked in a hot oven (200°C / 400°F / gas mark 6), the tart sets very quickly and the buttery, lemony mixture caramelizes slightly. It is probably one of the lightest tarts ever created.

## *Orange*

ORANGE

The orange, fruit of the gardens of the Hesperides, was offered as a gift to the King of France by Eleonora of Castille in the late seventeenth

A freshly picked orange

In an attic near Grenoble, the walnut oil press

century. A special glass-house was built so that the fruit could mature, and the fashion of the *orangerie* was set. Today, if the *orangerie* is still used in some châteaux, the citrus fruit and its hybrids grow wild in most gardens of the Mediterranean. The fruit which was once the exclusive pleasure of the rich and the Christmas dream of the pauper is now the most widely consumed fruit in France, all year round and especially in the winter.

The recipe for orange marmalade has been copied from the British Isles, although in France it is still called *confiture d'orange*, and is often served at breakfast to balance the buttery consistency of croissant. Orange tarts are baked with fine *pâte sablée,* served in wafer-thin slices with tea or with a meringue topping for dessert. The orange *baba* is a yeast cake on to which fresh orange juice is poured while still hot. In *nouvelle cuisine* the orange finds itself in salads, cooked with *coquille St-Jacques* or mixed with a fine butter as a sauce for turbot or halibut.

*Canard à l'orange* should in fact be called *canard à la bigarade,* which is the French denomination for Seville oranges. It will always remain one of the French classic dishes. The simplest way to prepare it is to place a peeled Seville orange in the cavity of the duck and roast in a moderate oven (180°C / 350°F / gas mark 4). At the end, the zest, which has been blanched to avoid any bitter taste, is added to the cooking juices along with the juices of the orange which cooked with the bird. Add a touch of Armagnac to the sauce, let it thicken naturally and serve in a gravy-boat with the carved bird, which has been quickly glazed with a small quantity of lemon and honey. Never use Cointreau or Curaçao and above all never glaze the duck with marmalade, for it is only the addition of the fresh fruit which will give this dish its fine taste.

Clementines and mandarines are mainly used in fresh fruit salad although they make delightful petits fours when dipped in a light caramel and left to dry. The small kumquat is often glazed with sugar and served with dark chocolate to accompany after-dinner coffee.

## Nuts

### *Amande*

ALMOND

The ethereal pink bloom of the almond tree intimates the first warm days of Provence or the Languedoc. Later on, the velvety, pale green fruit will form and the nuts eaten with brown bread and butter or dried for use in all sorts of sweet preparations, like *tartelettes amandines* which so inspired Edmond Rostand that he gave the recipe in verse in *Cyrano de Bergerac.*

*Frangipane,* a butter and almond paste, is used as a filling for the delicious Pithiviers, made with puff pastry, which is traditionally eaten in France for Epiphany. Fresh almond flavours the early recipe for *blancmanger* given by the illustrious cookery author and chef Taillevent in his book *Viandier,* written in the fourteenth century.

To accompany drinks, try preparing home-made salted almonds: fry blanched almonds in a little butter and spice with salt, cayenne pepper and a hint of fresh ginger. Dry on kitchen paper and serve warm or cold.

*Hazelnuts*

## *Châtaigne*

CHESTNUT

For centuries, the chestnut was a staple in the diet of countrymen from the Cévennes to the Massif Central. Chestnuts were boiled, then puréed and mixed with milk to make a soup flavoured with wild fennel and rosemary. Today, chestnuts are the traditional accompaniment of the Christmas turkey. In the Nivernais, boiled and peeled chestnuts are baked in an earthenware crock with bacon, herbs and prunes. Delicious with a salad of lamb's lettuce, this makes a fine main course for luncheon.

Chestnut log is one of the traditional French Christmas desserts. The nuts are puréed and mixed with melted dark chocolate, butter, walnut kernels, hazelnuts and almonds. The mixture is poured into a loaf tin and kept refrigerated for 12 hours. It can be served with whipped cream or a *crème anglaise.* The same mixture can be rolled into truffles and coated with unsweetened cocoa.

In the Limousin a mousse is made with chestnuts, egg whites and cream, served ice-cold inside meringue nests or in a glass cup with vanilla-flavoured whipped cream – *crème chantilly.*

Known also as *marron,* the chestnut is glazed in sugar as an after-dinner delicacy. This is a time-consuming preparation and *marrons glacés* have become the end-of-the-year speciality of many smart *pâtisseries.*

## *Noisette*

HAZELNUT

The *noisettier* or *coudrier* grows in a corner of most French gardens. The nut is at its best in September, when fresh, and is used for similar preparations as the walnut. Ground hazelnuts are mixed into a meringue, baked and filled with a purée of raspberries. Like almonds, hazelnuts can be sautéed in butter and spices to be served with drinks, and hazelnut butter is particularly fine with baked trout.

The best French variety is the cobnut known as *aveline*.

## *Noix*

WALNUT

Gardener, beware where you choose to plant your walnut tree! It will reach up to 20 m (60 ft) and the roots, which are the most developed of all fruit trees, exude a substance which is toxic enough to kill apple and pear trees, potatoes and tomatoes in a radius of 10 m (30 ft) around the tree.

Epicurian, beware! The walnut is so gorged with oil that it is extremely fattening: 100 g / 4 oz walnuts are the equivalent of 660 calories. Walnuts grow throughout France, although they are best around Grenoble and in the Périgord, and eaten in moderation, are good from apéritif to dessert, adding sophistication to the simplest of salads. The taste of walnut mixes intimately with any blue

*Nuts, ready to be used in a variety of sweet and savoury dishes*

cheese, and features in many recipes for tarts and cakes. Pound a few kernels with butter, core an apple and spoon the mixture into the cavity, then bake the fruit on a piece of buttered walnut bread in a slow oven. The nutty flavours caramelize with the butter and the apple juices, coating the bread which stays moist and delicious with the warm apple pulp. Dare I mention that a touch of single cream poured over the top adds to the delicacy?

Walnut kernels are a good addition to stuffings for chicken and turkey; they mix well with courgettes and smoked salmon as a sauce for fresh tagliatelle, and are excellent mixed with Roquefort cheese, inside a baked potato.

The green outer skin of fresh walnuts makes a wine which is much sought after in Provence, and the freshly pressed oil is excellent in the dressing of green salads, red cabbage, and even seafood such as squid or *coquilles-St-Jacques.*

For true gourmandizing try this little sandwich of my childhood: fresh walnut kernels, brown sugar and butter on brown bread.

Among the best French varieties look for: La Mayette, large and slightly oblong; La Franquette, a large indigenous species from the Périgord; La Corne, a small nut, full of flavour, which makes the best oil; and the Grandjean, round and pale and easy to separate into kernels.

# *The Château de St-Paterne*

After researching in depth the fascinating history of herbs, fruits and vegetables, I left my books and set off one spring morning on an unforgettable meandering journey through the kitchen gardens of France. I retraced my steps through most of the regions I had already visited for my previous book, *The Frenchwoman's Kitchen.* From the temperate North and Normandy to the luscious bounty of Provence, I helped gather the yield of gardens groomed by amateurs and professionals from early spring to autumn.

Shared enthusiasm for the growing of plants was followed by equally absorbing times spent in French kitchens, creating or reproducing family recipes with each harvest. From the earliest radish to the cabbages of winter I learned a great deal from attentive gardeners and inventive cooks. Above all, I shared the Frenchwoman's most passionate pride: the art of turning home-grown produce into culinary delights.

At St-Paterne near Alençon, delphiniums, larkspurs and foxgloves herald a world of leguminous extravagance and cornucopian fantasy. Charles Henry de Valbray, the youngest châtelain in France, has entrusted the running of his vegetable garden to a team of Laotian gardeners.

When Charles Henry inherited the ancestral estate nine years ago, the whole property was sadly

*A riot of flowers line the way to the château*

*Freshly picked mirabelle, an indigenous French plum*

neglected. The château, which had once been the love nest of Henri IV, was in serious need of repairs; the surrounding parkland and woods were totally overgrown. A man of infectious enthusiasm and exquisite taste, Charles Henry, who wished to open his home to guests, set to work.

While the rooms were restored, exposing historical paintings on walls and ceilings, the park was cleared to reveal stone walls clad with old-fashioned pear trees, a large *orangerie,* a herb terrace and a rose garden. The old fruit trees, informally dispersed around the lawns, were pruned and given new life. Today, antique garden chairs are set under the arboreal shade of rare species such as the large purple Pedigron plum, the original greengage, Reine-Claude, and an indigenous pear of the region: la Poire d'Alençon. Such fruits are served for dessert at the château throughout the summer months.

The vast sweep of land leading to the woods was barren and the ideal spot for a *potager.* Charles Henry designed the grass alleys which divide up the garden. From the château the *potager* has the aspect of any seventeenth-century kitchen garden, surrounded by tall herbaceous borders. The Laotians from the nearby town of Alençon are hard at work. The results are astonishing and the flavours brought to the kitchen quite unexpected, deep in the heart of Normandy.

It is late August. Pushing a large wheelbarrow, we have taken a walk through this Asian paradise. Organically grown, the vegetables twine round elaborate structures with refined complicity.

There is a bewildering collection of cucurbitae: squash, marrow, *marron* marrow, spaghetti marrow, siam marrows, yellow and deep orange pumpkins, courgettes, and all kinds of cucumbers and melons. In this jungle of gourds, some grow on stakes so that their leaves may protect the fine courgette flowers and more fragile plants from the direct sun and attack by insects.

We have picked a pumpkin for tonight's soup as well as an amazing dark green and white turban squash. Once hollowed, it will become the natural vessel of our lunch-time rice salad. Large courgette flowers will decorate the serving platter.

The choice for salads is immense. Chinese *pé-tsaï, daïkon* – a radish from Japan – chick-weed, garden cress, summer purslane, salad rocket, tiny cucumbers and peppers as well as wild mushrooms grown under cover by the wood. We decide to add the Chinese black bean which will look particularly attractive among the other vegetables.

The tomato patch is near the herb garden. The huge Marmande tomatoes are ripe, and Charles Henry insists on picking some to prepare a Southern recipe from Toulon, his second home.

Back in the kitchen, we realize that we have picked rather a lot of gourds. We will eat them all the same. And while Charles Henry starts his own recipe for pumpkin soup, I shall prepare our exotic salad, and tonight we will share a pumpkin soufflé with an orange and angelica sauce that I have been dying to cook for months.

## Lunch

# Salade de Riz d'Été

SUMMER RICE SALAD

*This salad was served inside the turban marrow we picked, but can be presented in any attractive large salad bowl.*

*For the Vinaigrette*
2 teaspoons salt
a large pinch of cayenne pepper
1 teaspoon freshly ground black pepper
1 teaspoon paprika
½ teaspoon curry powder
1 teaspoon Dijon mustard
3 tablespoons tarragon vinegar
3 tablespoons olive oil
2 tablespoons sunflower oil
2 basil leaves, torn
4 stems chervil, chopped
4 nasturtium leaves, chopped

*For the Salad*
500 g / 1 lb brown rice
10 cherry tomatoes
1 red pepper, seeded and peeled
1 green pepper, seeded and peeled
a handful of black French dwarf beans
a handful of young mange-tout
4 mushrooms, thinly sliced
50 g / 2 oz green olives, pitted
10 radishes, sliced
to decorate: some freshly picked courgette flowers
1 cucumber, peeled and cubed
and any other salad vegetables available in the kitchen garden at the time
12 quail's eggs

*To serve*
1 large marrow, hollowed
courgette or nasturtium flowers and leaves

*Serves 4*

Prepare the vinaigrette in advance to let the flavours mingle and develop. Mix all the ingredients together and whisk well.

Cook the rice in plenty of boiling salted water until tender and rinse well under a hot tap. Drain the rice and leave to cool. Mix some of the vinaigrette with the rice to moisten it well. Arrange the rice, vegetables and quail's eggs inside the hollowed marrow and decorate with courgette or nasturtium flowers and leaves.

*If marrows have inspired the ceramist, they should inspire the cook: here, a rice salad is served inside a marrow*

## Dinner

### *Soupe au Potiron de St-Paterne*

PUMPKIN SOUP

1 kg / 2 lb whole pumpkin
75 g / 3 oz butter
2 large onions, sliced
2 garlic cloves, sliced
125 ml / 4 fl oz full-bodied white wine
250 ml / 8 fl oz milk
600 ml / 1 pint chicken stock
salt and pepper
1 tablespoon chopped parsley
1 tablespoon chopped chives
juice of 1 orange
a dash of Tabasco
a dash of Worcestershire sauce
2 tablespoons double cream
150 g / 5 oz herb croûtons, to serve

*Serves 6*

Cut a large slice off the top of the pumpkin to use as a lid. Remove seeds and fibres from inside the pumpkin and carefully scoop out and reserve the flesh, leaving enough against the outer skin to form a hard shell. Set aside and cover with a damp tea-cloth.

Cube the pumpkin flesh. Melt the butter in a large saucepan and sauté the pumpkin with the onions and garlic until limp. Add the wine, milk and stock. Season with salt and pepper. Simmer gently for 45 minutes or until the vegetables are tender. Using a slotted spoon, transfer the vegetables to a food mill or blender and purée, gradually adding the cooking liquid a little at a time.

Return the purée to the pan. Stir in more of the remaining cooking liquid until the desired consistency is obtained. Add the parsley and chives, the orange juice, Tabasco and Worcestershire sauce. Check the seasoning. Stir in the cream and pour the soup inside the pumpkin shell. Serve at once with herb croûtons.

*Ripe pumpkins*

### *Soufflé au Potiron Caramélisé avec sauce à l'Orange et à l'Angélique*

CARAMELIZED PUMPKIN SOUFFLÉ WITH ORANGE AND ANGELICA SAUCE

500 g / 1 lb pumpkin
a pinch of salt
200 ml / 7 fl oz milk
1 vanilla pod, halved
50 g / 2 oz unsalted butter, softened
4 tablespoons caster sugar
1 tablespoon plain flour
1 tablespoon cornflour
½ teaspoon finely grated orange rind
2 eggs
1 egg white

*Wheelbarrow loaded with late summer gourds*

*For the Soufflé Dish*
25 g / 1 oz unsalted butter
1 heaped tablespoon caster sugar

*For the Sauce*
juice of 2 oranges
1 tablespoon Grand Marnier
½ teaspoon finely grated orange rind
25 g / 1 oz caster sugar
1 angelica leaf, finely chopped
15 g / ½ oz butter

*Serves 6*

Peel and dice the pumpkin. Place in a saucepan, cover with boiling water, add a pinch of salt and cook until tender. Drain very thoroughly.

Place the milk in a saucepan with the vanilla pod and scald. Leave to infuse for a few minutes, then discard the pod.

Transfer the pumpkin pulp to a mixing bowl and mash well with a fork or a potato masher. Add the butter and draw in with a spatula, then add the sugar and finally sift in the flour and cornflour. Work all the ingredients together.

Now, gradually work in the infused milk, a little at a time. Add the orange rind and leave to cool.

Separate the eggs and reserve the whites in a deep bowl. Work the egg yolks into the pumpkin mixture, one at a time.

Preheat the oven to 220°C / 425°F / gas mark 7. Butter a large soufflé dish, sprinkle some caster sugar over the base and sides and tap off the excess. Whisk the egg white until stiff. Add a quarter of the whisked whites to the pumpkin mixture, stir lightly until well mixed, then fold in the remaining whites as delicately as possible.

Bake the soufflé in the heated oven for 15–20 minutes or until well puffed and golden-brown.

While the soufflé is cooking, make the sauce. Pour the orange juice into a small saucepan together with the Grand Marnier, orange rind, sugar and angelica leaf. Bring to the boil, then lower the heat and allow to reduce slightly.

Cut the butter into small pieces. With the pan over a low heat, gradually whisk in the butter until the sauce is smooth and thick. Keep warm.

To serve the soufflé: heat the grill until very hot. Remove the soufflé from the oven, sprinkle immediately with sugar and place under the hot grill until caramelized. Serve at once, with the orange sauce passed in a sauce-boat.

## *Tartines Grillées aux Tomates et Poivrons*

COUNTRY TOAST WITH FRESH TOMATOES AND RED PEPPERS

4 large slices of country bread
2 garlic cloves, peeled
2 large tomatoes, peeled
marinated red peppers (see below)
salt and pepper

*Serves 4*

Toast the bread on both sides until brown and very crisp. Rub it immediately with the garlic, then the tomatoes, which will leave their fine pulp on the bread. Garnish with fine slivers of marinated peppers and a good sprinkling of salt and freshly ground black pepper.

These would make a delicious accompaniment to the rice salad, together with a good château wine.

## *Conserve de Poivrons à l'Huile*

MARINATED PEPPERS

1 bottle of good olive oil
1 stem rosemary
1 stem thyme, leaves and flowers
1 bay leaf
a few fennel seeds
a few coriander seeds
a few black peppercorns
zest of 1 lemon
4 garlic cloves
1 kg / 2 lb red peppers

A month in advance, prepare the oil. Add all the herbs, spices, lemon zest and garlic to the olive oil and leave to infuse in a cool place.

To prepare the peppers: cut them in half and discard the seeds. Place them on a baking tray, cut side down, and grill them until the skin is charred. Place the grilled peppers in a polythene bag, then peel off the skins, cut the flesh into fine strips and pack tightly into a preserving jar. Cover with the well-flavoured oil and seal tightly. They will keep for several months.

*An astonishing mixture of flowers and vegetables*

# A Day in the Orchard

Françoise and Klaus live an artistic idyll in the folds of the Suisse Normande, a hilly region of Southern Normandy. She is a dedicated gardener and a keen cook, and he is a born musician and an accomplished pianist. Life revolves around peace, music and self-sufficiency.

Their small cottage is set in an orchard. A vine and an old quince tree clamber over the stone walls and the garden is mainly laid out with vegetables and salad leaves as well as a few flowers such as nasturtium and borage that Françoise adds to salads and vegetable dishes. The herb patch is small but packed. In the far corner, hens pick freely at the ground.

When I arrived, Françoise was busy planting young leeks and lamb's lettuce. She explained that she only plants things when the moon is on the rise, an old Norman belief inherited from her grandfather.

Lunch was set on an antique cloth under the apple trees, cider was poured into glasses brought back by Klaus from Egypt after a concert there. We ate a *brouillade de Beaufort à la crème fleurette* – eggs scrambled with cheese and cream. With it, a *chiffonnade de trois salades aux champignons* – a fresh and herby mixed salad just picked from the garden – and, to crown it all, Françoise had baked small and fragrant herby muffins, her favourite picnic bread recipe.

*Harvested apples in the orchard*

In the evening, the weather was good enough to have a candle-lit dinner on the grass. The delectable menu started with a *potage au cerfeuil,* a light chervil soup, then rabbit's legs stuffed with an amazing herby mixture. We finished with a speciality from the region – a pear baked inside the thinnest of puff pastry.

## Lunch

### Brouillade de Beaufort à la Crème Fleurette

CREAMY SCRAMBLED EGGS

8 large eggs
3 tablespoons single cream
50 g / 2 oz Beaufort or Gruyère cheese, grated
100 g / 4 oz butter

*Serves 6*

Beat the eggs with the cream. Add the grated cheese and salt to taste. Melt the butter in a heavy-based non-stick pan over a medium heat. Pour in the egg mixture. Stir until just set but still creamy.

### Chiffonnade aux Champignons

HERB AND MUSHROOM SALAD

25 g / 1 oz butter
2 teaspoons sunflower oil
200 g / 7 oz mushrooms, thinly sliced
200 g / 7 oz lamb's lettuce
1 large lettuce heart
1 oak-leaf lettuce
12 walnut kernels
1 apple, diced

*For the vinaigrette*

1½ teaspoons sherry vinegar
3 tablespoons walnut oil
1 teaspoon finely chopped chervil
1 teaspoon finely chopped chives

*Serves 4*

Heat the butter and oil in a frying pan and sauté the mushrooms until lightly browned.

While the mushrooms are cooking, wash and trim the three salad leaves. Shake off the excess water and arrange in a salad bowl with the walnuts and apple.

Make the vinaigrette by combining all the ingredients. Pour over the salad and toss well. Lay the warm mushrooms on top and serve at once.

### Muffins aux Herbes

HERB MUFFINS

100 g / 4 oz butter
2 eggs
1 teaspoon finely chopped tarragon
1 teaspoon finely chopped chervil
1 teaspoon finely chopped chives
½ garlic clove, crushed
salt and pepper
150 g / 5 oz plain flour
1 teaspoon baking powder
15 g / ½ oz butter, for greasing

*Makes 8*

Preheat the oven to 200°F / 400°C / gas mark 6. Melt the butter over a very low heat. Beat the eggs lightly. Off the heat, stir the eggs, herbs, garlic, salt and pepper into the melted butter.

Sift the flour with the baking powder and add to the egg mixture. Work lightly with a spatula until the mixture is smooth.

Grease 8 muffin tins and spoon in the mixture. Bake in the heated oven for 25–30 minutes or until a skewer inserted into the centre of a muffin comes out clean. Serve lukewarm or cold.

## Dinner

### *Potage au Cerfeuil*

CHERVIL SOUP

1 kg / 2 lb potatoes
600 ml / 1 pint water
1 very large bunch of freshly picked chervil
100 g / 4 oz crème fraîche
50 g / 2 oz butter
salt and pepper

*Serves 6*

Peel the potatoes, wash them well and cut into thick slices. Cook in a saucepan of boiling salted water for 15–20 minutes or until tender.

Meanwhile wash the chervil carefully, shake off the excess water and cut up finely with scissors. Purée the potatoes in a food processor or liquidizer, adding the cooking liquid a little at a time.

Return the soup to the pan, add the chopped chervil and leave to infuse for 2 minutes. Stir well and check the seasoning. Stir in the butter and crème fraîche over a very low heat. Serve as soon as the butter has melted.

*Chervil soup*

### *Cuisses de Lapin Farcies aux Herbes*

RABBIT'S THIGHS WITH A HERB STUFFING

6 large rabbit's thighs
3 slices of smoked raw ham
225 g / 8 oz young spinach leaves
6 young sorrel leaves
1 sage leaf
1 teaspoon finely chopped parsley
1 teaspoon finely chopped chives
350 g / 12 oz finely ground veal or pork
1 onion, chopped
1 large shallot, chopped
1 garlic clove, chopped
1 egg
salt and pepper
25 g / 1 oz butter
2 tablespoons olive oil
4 shallots, peeled but left whole
500 g / 1 lb wild mushrooms
150 ml / 5 fl oz full-bodied white Burgundy

*Serves 6*

*A light herb stuffing for this rabbit fricassée*

Using the blade of a sharp thin kitchen knife, carefully bone the rabbit's thigh, leaving the upper leg as it is. Open the meat up and lay half a slice of ham inside each thigh.

Wash the spinach and sorrel carefully. Shake off all excess water, dry with kitchen paper and chop finely. Chop the sage leaf. Mix the vegetables with the mixed parsley and chives. Place the ground meat, onion, shallot and garlic in a mixing bowl with the spinach, sorrel and fresh herbs. Beat the egg with a little salt and pepper and add to the mixture. Mix well with a fork, then with your hands.

Carefully spoon the stuffing inside each rabbit's thigh. Truss securely with needle and thread.

Heat the butter and oil in a flameproof casserole and sauté the rabbit pieces on all sides until brown. Add the shallots, mushrooms, wine and seasoning. Cover, reduce the heat and simmer for 50–60 minutes, turning the rabbit pieces from time to time. Add a little water if the cooking juices reduce too much, although the sauce should just coat the meat. Check the seasoning.

Serve with steamed new potatoes and the juices from the pan.

## Poires en Chemise

PEARS WRAPPED IN THIN PUFF PASTRY

*Choose firm pears which are sweet and fragrant so that no sugar needs to be added. The natural sweetness of the fruit will caramelize inside the light pastry. The quality of the pastry is also very important, as the buttery taste adds to the simple excellence of this dessert.*

6 large fragrant pears

*For the pastry*

200 g / 7 oz strong white flour
a pinch of salt
150 g / 5 oz fine unsalted butter
125 ml / 4 fl oz iced water
1 egg yolk, to glaze

*Serves 6.*

To make the pastry: sift the flour and salt on to a large wooden board. Make a well in the centre of the flour. Cut 15 g / ½ oz of the butter into tiny pieces and dot them over the flour. Pour the iced water into the well in the centre. Working quickly with cool fingertips, work the butter into the flour, then draw the flour into the water until a dough is formed. Knead 2–3 times with the palms of your hands until the dough is smooth.

Roll the dough into an oblong about 5 mm / ¼ in thick. Place the remaining butter between 2 sheets of greaseproof paper and roll it with a rolling pin until it is pliable. The butter should have more or less the same thickness and consistency as the dough. Remove the paper. Divide the butter into small pieces and place at the centre of the dough.

Fold each of the 4 pastry sides over the butter so that the butter is completely enclosed. Leave to rest in a cool room for 10 minutes.

Place the dough on the board, joins upwards. Flatten slightly with a rolling pin, then roll out to an oblong about 5 mm / ¼ in thick.

Turn the dough so that the short end is facing you. Fold the bottom third over towards the middle, then the top third down over the folded third, just as you would fold a napkin. Leave to rest in a cool room for 15 minutes.

Return the dough to the board, roll out into the same oblong as before and fold in three again. Chill for a further 15 minutes.

Repeat the rolling, folding and chilling another 4 times. After chilling for the last time, the pastry will be extremely light and ready to roll out.

Preheat the oven to 220°C / 425°F / gas mark 7.

Peel the pears, leaving them whole with the stem on. Using a fruit corer, core each pear from the base.

Roll out the pastry as thinly as possible and divide into 6 squares, each large enough to allow the wrapping of a whole fruit.

Pat each pear dry with kitchen paper and place at the centre of each pastry square. Fold the pastry edges towards the stem, following the shape of the fruit. Make a twist at the top to secure. From the remaining pastry, cut out some leaf shapes and fix them by the pear stems. Seal the edges by moistening each side of the pastry, then pressing together. Brush with the egg yolk beaten with a little water.

Place on a lightly moistened baking tray and bake in the heated oven for 30 minutes, reducing the heat slightly if the pastry shows signs of over-browning. Serve the pears on their own while still hot.

*Poires en Chemise: a speciality from the region*

# A Tamed Wilderness in the Rouergue

In the Rouergue, a small enclave of Gascony, the mountainous landscape is harsh and only the natural pungent ground-covering of thyme, oregano and summer savory seems to thrive.

When Adèle, who is a teacher, moved with her boyfriend to an abandoned shepherd's house on a small south-facing plateau, the challenge they faced was to make use of their long holidays to tame the natural wilderness and create a garden where the bright colours of Southern flowers, fruit and vegetables would play with the beaming sun and trees and bushes would create enough shade to defy the fiery summer heat.

Today, broom, lilies, old-fashioned roses and honey-scented flowering laurel line the path to a small *potager* where melons, large tomatoes, peppers and aubergines ripen freely.

To sit on the shady terrace which looks on to the valley below is paradisical. In the evening, the perfumes of the garden mix with the natural fragrance of the stark surrounding hillsides, combining with the wine and the excellent food in an intoxicating revelation of senses.

Lunch started with a salad of Roquefort, the local cheese. To follow, Adèle prepared her speciality, a squash stuffed with chicken, cooked in a strong tomato sauce. We finished with a recipe we invented: a medley of fresh and dried fruits served ice-cold on a yoghurt and honey sauce, and

*Large summer leaves defy the fiery heat*

impregnated with the unique flavour of the local Armagnac. This dessert would now be called *les poires d'Adèle,* for it is she who planted the apricot and pear trees against the house, and the prunes are dried naturally in the sun by one of her aunts in the Lot valley.

In the evening we shared a baked speciality from the region, *farçun du Rouergue,* and finished with a surprising combination of melon and large raspberries topped with a lemony meringue.

I left with one of their favourite soup recipes, which I looked forward to trying on colder days: *soupe au farci périgourdin,* a hearty soup made by the aunt who dries the prunes.

## Lunch

### *Salade de Frisée au Roquefort*

ENDIVE SALAD WITH ROQUEFORT CHEESE

75 g / 3 oz Roquefort cheese
2 tablespoons single cream
½ teaspoon Dijon mustard
1 teaspoon lemon juice
2 teaspoons olive oil
salt and pepper
1 *frisée* endive
1 tablespoon chopped chervil
1 teaspoon chopped tarragon
12 walnut kernels

*Serves 4*

In a salad bowl, mash the Roquefort cheese with the cream. Add the mustard, lemon juice and olive oil. Season with salt and pepper.

Wash, trim and dry the *frisée.* Discard the dark green outer leaves, keeping only the white leaves.

*Endive and winter Brassica*

Transfer to the salad bowl. Sprinkle with the herbs. Toss well and garnish with walnut kernels.

### *Pâtisson Farci au Poulet*

SQUASH STUFFED WITH SPICY CHICKEN

500 g / 1 lb chicken breasts, skinned
1 tablespoon olive oil
1 tablespoon chopped onion
2 garlic cloves, chopped
2 tomatoes, peeled and chopped
1 tablespoon chopped fennel
1 tablespoon tomato purée
150 ml / 5 fl oz dry white wine
1 bouquet garni (bay leaf, rosemary, sage)
salt and pepper
1 squash
75 g / 3 oz Gruyère cheese, grated

*Serves 4*

Cut the chicken into small cubes. Heat the oil in a frying pan and sauté the chicken on all sides until browned. Add the onion and garlic and sauté until limp and transparent. Now add the tomatoes, fennel and tomato purée. Pour in the wine, season with salt and pepper and add the *bouquet garni*. Cover and reduce the heat to simmering point. Cook for 40 minutes, stirring from time to time. If the cooking juices have not reduced enough towards the end of cooking time, uncover the pan. The sauce must just coat the meat.

Meanwhile, using a small sharp knife, cut a round lid off the top of the squash. Spoon out the seeds and fibres. Place the squash in boiling water and cook for 15 minutes or until the flesh is tender. Drain well, upside down in a colander.

Preheat the oven to 220°C / 425°F / gas mark 7.

Spoon the chicken mixture into the squash. Sprinkle with grated cheese and bake in the heated oven until the cheese begins to melt. Serve at once.

## *Les Poires d'Adèle*

ADÈLE'S PEARS

6 large prunes, stoned
75 ml / 3 fl oz Armagnac
6 ripe apricots
6 fresh blanched almonds
6 large firm pears
600 ml / 1 pint water
thinly pared zest of 1 lemon
1 vanilla pod, halved
1 small cinnamon stick
300 ml / 10 fl oz plain Greek yoghurt
1 tablespoon clear honey
1 tablespoon chopped fresh pistachios

*Serves 6*

*Chicken pieces baked in squash*

*A favourite corner in Adèle's garden*

Soak the prunes overnight in the Armagnac. Stone the apricots and replace each stone with an almond.

Peel the pears, leaving the stems. Cut a thin slice from the base of each pear and stand them upright in a saucepan. Add the water, lemon zest, vanilla pod and cinnamon and cook, covered, over a very low heat until the pears are just tender. Leave to cool in the saucepan.

Lift the pears from the syrup and leave to drain. Core the pears from the base. Using a slotted spoon, lift the prunes from the Armagnac. Fill each prune with an almond-stuffed apricot and push the mixed fruit inside the pear. Refrigerate.

To serve: mix the yoghurt with the honey and spread over individual dessert plates. Stand a pear in the centre of each plate and decorate the sauce with the pistachios. Serve with home-made *tuiles* or *cigarettes russes.*

## Dinner

### *Farçun du Rouergue*

BACON AND VEGETABLE BAKE

1 kg / 2 lb spinach
3 celery stalks with leaves
200 g / 7 oz smoked rindless streaky bacon
1 tablespoon chopped parsley
2 garlic cloves, crushed
1 stem fresh thyme
black pepper
400 ml / 14 fl oz milk
1 bay leaf
a pinch of freshly grated nutmeg
100 g / 4 oz butter
60 g / 2½ oz plain flour
3 eggs
2 tablespoons crème fraîche
a sheet of caul fat the size of the dish (ask your butcher to prepare this)

*Serves 6*

Wash the spinach in plenty of water. Wash the celery and remove the large strings from the stalks. Finely chop the spinach, celery leaves and stalks and mix.

Mince the bacon with the parsley and garlic cloves. Add the thyme leaves and season with freshly ground black pepper.

Preheat the oven to 180°C / 350°F / gas mark 4.

Prepare a béchamel sauce. Scald the milk in a saucepan with the bay leaf, nutmeg and a touch of black pepper. Leave to infuse for 10 minutes.

Melt 75 g / 3 oz of the butter in a heavy-based saucepan, then work in the flour over a very low heat, stirring constantly. Gradually strain in the hot milk and bring the sauce to the boil. Lower the heat and simmer, stirring all the time, for 4-5 minutes or until the sauce thickens. Remove from the heat and leave to cool slightly.

Beat the eggs with the crème fraîche and slowly pour into the cooled béchamel sauce. Stir the bacon and vegetables into the sauce and check seasoning.

Grease an earthenware dish with the remaining butter and pour in the mixture. Soak the caul fat in tepid water to make it pliable. Spread over the surface of the dish. Bake in the heated oven for 45–50 minutes or until set. Serve warm, cut into squares.

### *Chaudfroid de Melon Meringué*

FRENCH MELON WITH A MERINGUE TOPPING

3 Charentais or Cavaillon melons, chilled
300 g / 10 oz raspberries
100 g / 4 oz caster sugar

*For the meringue*
4 egg whites
½ teaspoon lemon juice
½ teaspoon finely grated lemon rind
6 tablespoons caster sugar

*Serves 6*

Preheat the oven to 220°C / 425°F / gas mark 7.

Halve each melon crosswise and remove the seeds and fibres as well as the excess juice.

Wrap each half of the melon in a square of kitchen foil, without covering the top. (The foil will prevent the melon from cooking while in the oven.)

Toss the raspberries in the sugar and spoon them inside the melon halves.

Whisk the egg whites until stiff. Gradually add the lemon juice, rind and sugar. Pile the meringue over the fruit and place in the heated oven for a few minutes until the meringue topping is golden.

## Soupe au Farci Périgourdin

THICK SOUP FROM THE PÉRIGORD

*For the farci*
200 ml / 7 fl oz chicken stock
300 g / 10 oz country bread, crusts removed
3 eggs
200 g / 7 oz unsmoked streaky bacon in one piece
2 garlic cloves
2 shallots
1 onion
1 tablespoon chopped chives
salt and pepper
a pinch of freshly grated nutmeg
6 large cabbage leaves

*For the soup*
25 g / 1 oz butter
25 g / 1 oz duck or goose fat
2 leeks, sliced
2 carrots, sliced
1 large turnip, sliced
1 large onion, quartered
1 large clove of garlic, sliced
1 litre / 1¾ pints chicken stock
100 g / 4 oz small green beans, topped and tailed
200 g / 7 oz shelled haricot beans
2 large tomatoes, peeled, seeded and chopped
salt and pepper
1 bay leaf

First make the *farci*: warm the chicken stock and soak the bread until soft. Squeeze out the excess liquid and mash the bread with a fork in a mixing bowl. Work in the eggs, one at a time.

Mince the bacon, garlic, shallots and onion. Add the chives. Blend this mixture well with the bread in the bowl. Season with salt, pepper and nutmeg. Shape into a round dumpling in the bowl and chill.

Blanch the cabbage leaves in salted boiling water for 5 minutes. Drain the leaves well, pat dry and lay them flat over a wooden board. Wrap the dumpling in the cabbage leaves and tie the parcel securely with kitchen string.

To make the soup: melt the butter and duck or goose fat in a large saucepan. Add the leeks, carrots, turnip, onion and garlic and leave to sweat until transparent and limp. Pour in the chicken stock. Add the green beans, haricot beans and tomatoes. Season with salt and pepper and add the bay leaf. Bring to the boil and boil for a few minutes, then reduce the heat to simmering point. (If fresh haricot beans are not available, use dried: soak overnight before draining and adding to the soup.)

Lower the dumpling carefully into the saucepan. Cover and cook gently for 1 hour.

To serve: lift the dumpling from the pot and leave to cool slightly, then untie it and cut into thick slices. Pour the vegetable soup into a soup tureen and serve the sliced *farci* as a side dish with the soup.

*Herb-flavoured dumplings will be wrapped in cabbage leaves for the farci*

*Summer evening by the garden door*

# The Kitchen Garden in Bloom

Aliette's garden is a dazzling combination of flowers and vegetables. She left a large farmhouse with an orderly kitchen garden, orchards and fields, to live on a small town square in a village near Angers in the Loire Valley.

The walled garden which surrounds her house had mainly been laid out as terrace and lawns by the previous owners. 'There were a few dull everlasting bushes here and there,' says Aliette, 'but the garden lacked colour and I was determined to carry on enjoying the pleasure of fresh herbs and vegetables.

'To create a separate *potager* and ornamental garden,' she adds, 'would have been a visual disaster in the space available. So, one day, I closed my eyes and imagined the whole garden as if it had been planted by birds – seedlings of all kinds dropped in disarray, an intimate profusion of perfumes, colours and flavours. A garden which would please all five senses simultaneously.'

With care, good taste and abundant gardening knowledge (to which she refuses to admit), Aliette has transformed traditional French formality into an intricate tapestry of herbs, salad leaves, flowers and vegetables, woven together into a stunning design. Today, pinks and calendula mingle with lettuces, soft orange poppies grow profusely among flowering chives and sweet peas clamber up the tall stems of maize.

*Aliette's garden, a dazzling combination of flowers and vegetables*

*Artichoke in bloom*

This intricate filigree is the source of many healthy meals and creative flower arrangements for the cottage. I stayed two days with Aliette. The food was as delicate and imaginative as the surroundings.

For luncheon, Aliette and I made a soufflé of artichoke hearts mixed with small oyster mushrooms grown by the neighbours. It was followed by a French classic: *poulet à l'estragon*, a chicken fricassée with fresh tarragon. To finish, we ate a chilled terrine of peaches and raspberries.

In the evening, after a few glasses of chilled Loire wine, we prepared a lettuce soup, followed by a moist *omelette fermière aux poireaux* – an omelette filled with buttered young leeks – a recipe that Aliette had gathered from a friend on market day. Finally, a light raspberry mousse.

The day I left, we shared a complete vegetarian luncheon: first, a salad made with young spinach leaves and a *confit* of small onions; then *betteraves à la provençale* – large slices of freshly cooked beetroot sautéed in garlic butter and served with a fragrant purée of potatoes made with olive oil. A light *gratin* of apples baked in orange juice crowned this splendid garden luncheon.

## LUNCH

### *Soufflé d'Artichauts aux Pleurottes*

ARTICHOKE SOUFFLÉ WITH OYSTER MUSHROOMS

6 medium artichokes
6 small oyster mushrooms, chopped
3 thin slices of baked ham, chopped
1 tablespoon olive oil
4 tablespoons crème fraîche
salt and pepper
50 g / 2 oz slightly salted butter
2 tablespoons plain flour
250 ml / 8 fl oz milk
6 eggs
a pinch of freshly grated nutmeg

*Serves 6*

Discard the stalks and bottom leaves from the artichokes. Cook them in a saucepan of salted boiling water, heads down, for 30–45 minutes or until one of the leaves can be detached easily from the choke. As soon as they are cooked, transfer the artichokes to a colander, again heads down, run cold water over them and drain thoroughly.

Detach the artichoke leaves, one by one, scraping the flesh from the bottom of each leaf with a teaspoon. Discard the leaves. Place the flesh in a bowl.

Scoop out the hairy chokes and place each artichoke heart at the bottom of a buttered individual soufflé dish or ramekin.

Tie greaseproof paper around the outside of each dish to double its height. Secure with kitchen string.

Preheat the oven to 220°C / 425°F / gas mark 7.

Sauté the mushrooms and ham in oil until just golden but not brown. Transfer to the bowl containing the artichoke flesh and add 1 tablespoon of the crème fraîche. Season with salt and pepper.

Mix well and divide among the 6 dishes, spooning the mixture on to the artichoke hearts.

Now make a béchamel sauce. Melt the butter in a heavy-based saucepan and stir in the flour. Gradually add the milk, stirring all the time until the sauce is smooth and reaches boiling point. Now add the remaining crème fraîche. Take the pan off the heat and leave to cool slightly.

Separate the eggs. Keep the whites in a deep bowl and add the yolks one by one to the béchamel sauce, stirring well. Stir in the nutmeg and check the seasoning.

Whisk the egg whites until stiff and fold them delicately into the sauce. Spoon the mixture into each soufflé dish up to three-quarters of the total height, including the paper. Bake in the heated oven for 20–25 minutes or until well risen and just golden-brown. Serve at once.

## *Poulet à l'Estragon*

CHICKEN SAUTÉED WITH FRESH TARRAGON

1 large free-range chicken
salt and pepper
1 tablespoon sunflower oil
75 g / 3 oz butter
150 ml / 5 fl oz chicken stock
1 teaspoon lemon juice
2 tablespoons Noilly Prat
1 tablespoon chopped tarragon

*Serves 6*

Cut the chicken into 6–8 pieces. Season each piece with salt and pepper.

Heat the oil and 50 g / 2 oz of the butter in a flameproof casserole and brown the chicken pieces on all sides. Transfer the chicken to a plate. Pour off all but 1 tablespoon of the fat. Add the stock, lemon juice, Noilly Prat and the tarragon. Bring the sauce back to the boil, stirring well. Return the chicken pieces to the casserole. Cover and simmer for 50–60 minutes or until the chicken is cooked.

To serve: transfer the chicken pieces to a heated serving platter. Strain the sauce into a small saucepan and whisk in the remaining butter, a small piece at a time, until the sauce is smooth. Check the seasoning and pour the sauce over the chicken. Serve with new potatoes.

*Even the dullest wall is brightened up by the summer dahlias*

*Ripe peaches in the orchard*

## *Terrine de Pêches et Framboises*

CHILLED TERRINE OF PEACHES AND RASPBERRIES

100 g / 4 oz soft brown sugar
75 cl bottle rosé wine
1 vanilla pod, halved
a strip of thinly pared lemon zest
2 kg / 4 lb peaches or nectarines
500 g / 1 lb raspberries
2 teaspoons raspberry liqueur
25 g / 1 oz powdered gelatine
mint leaves, to decorate

*Serves 6*

Put the sugar, wine, vanilla pod and lemon zest into a large saucepan and heat, stirring, until the sugar is dissolved. Bring to the boil and cook, uncovered, for 8 minutes.

Peel the peaches or nectarines and cut them in half. Immerse them in the wine mixture in the saucepan and poach gently over a low heat until tender but still slightly firm. Remove from the heat and leave the peaches to cool in the syrup. Lift the peaches from the syrup and pat dry on a piece of kitchen paper. Discard the vanilla pod and lemon zest and set the syrup aside.

Roughly mash the raspberries with a fork. Layer peaches and mashed raspberries in a large oiled terrine mould. Sprinkle the gelatine over 3–4 tablespoons of the reserved syrup. Warm the remaining syrup slightly, then add the soaked gelatine and heat very gently, stirring, until the gelatine has dissolved completely. (On no account let the mixture boil.) Add the raspberry liqueur and pour over the fruit in the terrine. Chill for at least 4 hours, until set.

To serve: turn out the terrine on to a long serving platter. Decorate with mint leaves. Serve on its own or with single cream or thin plain yoghurt.

# DINNER

## *Velouté de Laitue*

LETTUCE SOUP

400 ml / 14 fl oz milk
1 litre / 1¾ pints water
salt and pepper
1 tablespoon chopped chives
1 teaspoon chopped parsley
1 teaspoon chopped chervil
2 large potatoes, sliced
2 round lettuces
75 g / 3 oz butter
2 tablespoons crème fraîche
1 egg yolk

*Serves 4*

In a large saucepan, bring the milk and water to the boil with salt and pepper. Add the herbs and potatoes and simmer over a very gentle heat until the potatoes are cooked.

Meanwhile, carefully wash the lettuces and shred them finely. Melt the butter in a large, heavy-based saucepan and sweat the lettuce for 5 minutes. Pour the herby milk and potatoes over the lettuce and bring to the boil. Check the seasoning and purée in a blender until very smooth.

Return the soup to the pan and bring to boiling point. Place the crème fraîche and egg yolk in a mixing bowl. Beat together and slowly whisk in a small amount of soup until thoroughly blended. Pour this mixture back into the saucepan, reduce the heat to the lowest point and stir gently and constantly until the soup starts to thicken. Serve at once, with warm crusty bread.

## Omelette Fermière à la Julienne de Poireau

OMELETTE WITH YOUNG BUTTERED LEEKS

4 young leeks
50 g / 2 oz butter
salt and pepper
8 eggs
1 teaspoon chopped chives
50 g / 2 oz Gruyère cheese, grated
1 tablespoon crème fraîche
4 thin slices of braised ham

*Serves 4*

Trim the leek and discard the toughest green leaves, leaving as much tender green as possible. Wash the leeks carefully under cold running water and slice them into fine, regular julienne strips.

Place half the butter in a heavy-based saucepan, cover with the leeks and leave to sweat over a low heat until they are tender, making sure they never take colour. When all the cooking liquid has evaporated, leave to cool slightly. Season with salt and pepper.

Whisk the eggs in a large bowl with the chives. Stir the leeks into the mixture.

Heat the remaining butter in a non-stick omelette pan over a medium heat. When the sizzling begins to die down, pour the egg mixture into the pan. As the mixture begins to set, draw it towards you, tilting the pan so that any liquid left sets underneath. Sprinkle the surface of the omelette with the grated cheese, spread over the crème fraîche with a spatula and continue cooking until the omelette is set to your liking.

To serve: slide the slices of braised ham into the omelette and fold in half over a heated serving platter. Serve at once.

## Mousse à la Framboise

RASPBERRY MOUSSE

500 g / 1 lb raspberries
1 tablespoon cornflour
juice of 2 oranges
3 eggs
200 g / 7 oz caster sugar
200 ml / 7 fl oz whipping cream

*To decorate*
single cream
raspberries
mint leaves

*Serves 4*

Purée and sieve the raspberries. Mix the cornflour with the orange juice and add to the raspberry pulp.

Separate the eggs. Place the whites in a deep bowl and set aside. In a mixing bowl, work the egg yolks with the sugar until pale and frothy. Work in the raspberry purée.

Transfer the mixture to a heavy-based saucepan and allow to thicken over the lowest possible heat, stirring constantly. When the mixture is thick enough to coat the back of a spoon, remove from the heat and leave to cool completely.

Whisk the egg whites until very stiff. Fold the whipped cream into the raspberry mixture, then fold in the whisked egg whites. Pour into individual moulds and chill for at least 6 hours until set. Serve with a touch of single cream poured over the top. Decorate with whole raspberries and mint leaves.

## Vegetarian Lunch

### Chiffonnade de Pousses d'Épinards au Confit d'Oignons

SALAD OF YOUNG SPINACH LEAVES WITH CARAMELIZED ONIONS

*Onions and beans on a garden step*

500 g / 1 lb small pickling onions, peeled
200 ml / 7 fl oz dry sherry
2 tablespoons olive oil
1 garlic clove, peeled and crushed
2 cloves
1 tablespoon sultanas
500 g / 1 lb young spinach leaves
12 walnut kernels
2 teaspoons soft brown sugar
1 teaspoon sherry vinegar
2 teaspoons chopped coriander leaves
salt and pepper

*For the vinaigrette*
2 tablespoons walnut oil
1 tablespoon sunflower oil
1 tablespoon sherry vinegar
salt and pepper

*Serves 4*

Heat the oil in a frying pan and sauté the onions until they start to take colour without browning. Add the sherry, garlic, cloves and sultanas and enough water to cover the onions. Partially cover the pan. Lower the heat and simmer gently until all the cooking liquid has evaporated. Discard the cloves.

Meanwhile, carefully wash the spinach leaves and dry them with kitchen paper. Place them in a large salad bowl. Combine all the ingredients for the vinaigrette and whisk well. Pour over the spinach and toss well, adding the walnut kernels.

To serve: over a medium heat, sprinkle the brown sugar over the onions and stir until the onions are caramelized. Add the vinegar and coriander leaves. Stir well. Check the seasoning and spoon the warm onions over the salad. Accompany with walnut bread (see page 96).

### Purée de Pommes de Terre à l'Huile d'Olive

POTATOES PURÉED WITH OLIVE OIL

1 kg / 2 lb floury potatoes
75 ml / 3 fl oz single cream
1 bay leaf
1 garlic clove
½ tablespoon olive oil
salt and pepper

*Serves 6*

Peel and quarter the potatoes. Cook in salted boiling water for 20 minutes or until tender. Scald the cream with the bay leaf and garlic and leave to infuse.

When the potatoes are cooked, drain and remove the bay leaf and garlic from the cream.

Mash the potatoes, gradually working in the cream. Check the seasoning. Warm the olive oil until tepid. Using a wooden spoon, beat the olive oil into the potato, a little at a time. Serve at once.

*Beetroot à la provençale*

## *Betteraves à la Provençale*

BEETROOT SAUTÉED IN GARLIC BUTTER

3 large beetroots, cooked and peeled
1 tablespoon olive oil
50 g / 2 oz butter
2 garlic cloves, crushed
1 tablespoon chopped parsley
1 tablespoon sour cream
1 teaspoon chopped chives
salt and pepper

*Serves 6*

Cut the beetroot into thick slices. Heat the oil and butter in a large frying pan and sauté the beetroot slices on both sides until sealed. Sprinkle the garlic and parsley over the beetroot. Check the seasoning. Add the sour cream to the pan juices with the chives. Serve at once.

## *Gratin de Pommes à l'Orange*

APPLE AND ORANGE GRATIN

6 large dessert apples
90 g / 3½ oz unsalted butter
200 g / 7 oz soft brown sugar
juice of 3 oranges

*Serves 6*

Preheat the oven to 220°C / 425°F / gas mark 7. Peel the apples. Core each one carefully with an apple corer. Cut crosswise into medium slices.

Grease the base of an earthenware baking dish with some of the butter. Lay in the apple slices, overlapping them slightly. Sprinkle the sugar over the fruit, pour in the orange juice and dot with the remaining butter. Bake in the oven until the apples are cooked and the juice bubbling and caramelized. Serve the gratin warm, on its own or with cream.

# Vines, Wine and the Kitchen Garden

*A gastronomic retreat in Provence*

Jacqueline looks after the vines and the wine. Adeline looks after the garden and the food. Their cousin looks after the goats and the cheese, and they all look after old Pape – Provençal for Papa – in a rambling priory near Vaison-la-Romaine and set on a mountainside which dominates the Rhône Valley.

The property is massive, with many acres of land, and because the vegetable garden had to be laid near water, down at the entrance to the track which leads to the *domaine*, there is no question of just popping outside for a tomato or a green pepper. One actually needs to make a list before walking the twenty minutes which separate the kitchen from a yield of Southern ripeness.

For herbs, it is easier. They grow on the terrace in ancient terracotta urns; the more delicate ones are to be found at the foot of the fig tree.

In the *potager*, melons sprawl over the ground, heavy and sweet-scented, ready to be picked. 'We'll have them for dessert,' says Adeline, 'filled with iced Beaume de Venise' – the natural sweet wine of the area, so full of the taste of Muscat grapes that it bites back.

*An original first course: tatin de tomates*

On our list we also have aubergines that will be used to make a gratin with goat's cheese and an anchovy sauce. Tomatoes will be needed too, of course. I will make a *tarte Tatin* with them, an excellent variation of the classic apple tart.

We cut a large bunch of Swiss chard to prepare *gayettes,* a local fresh sausage made with vegetables, pork, liver and herbs. And as the first haricot beans of the year are just ready, Adeline will make a bean and tomato soup. We dig a celeriac and some potatoes and walk back the stony track, planning menus for a couple of days.

With the celeriac we made a salad mixed with home-pickled olives prepared *à la tapénade.* It was followed by the aubergine gratin, then the melon.

For our late supper on the terrace we shared Adeline's delicious bean and tomato soup and some potato cakes baked with pesto. For dessert that night, we simply picked the first ripe grapes from the terrace.

The next meal was a concerted effort. I made the tomato tart, Adeline spent hours preparing the sumptuous *gayettes* which we ate with relish, accompanied by lots of Côtes du Rhône wine, and the two of us created a dessert of baked fresh figs with fresh goat's cheese that we served, with great pride, on a precious eighteenth-century Moustier serving platter.

## Lunch

### *Rémoulade de Céléri-rave au Tartare d'Olives*

CELERIAC AND BLACK OLIVE SALAD

1 head of celeriac
3 tablespoons olive oil
2 teaspoons lemon juice
1 teaspoon chopped coriander leaves
salt and pepper
200 g / 7 oz large pitted black olives
75 g / 3 oz anchovy fillets
100 g / 4 oz canned tuna, drained
1 teaspoon capers
2 teaspoons chopped chives

*To garnish*
1 lemon
flat-leaved parsley

*Serves 6*

Peel and grate the celeriac. Mix immediately with 2 tablespoons of the olive oil, the lemon juice, coriander and a little salt and pepper. Toss well.

Chop the olives with the anchovy fillets and the tuna. Mix in the capers, the remaining olive oil and the chives. Season with freshly ground black pepper.

Spoon the olive mixture into the centre of a round dish. Surround with the grated celeriac, in a crown shape. Decorate with lemon slices and parsley.

*Aubergines on Provençal stone*

### *Gratin d'Aubergines au Chèvre Frais*

AUBERGINE GRATIN WITH GOAT'S CHEESE

1 kg / 2 lb aubergines, sliced but not peeled
juice of 1 lemon
3 tablespoons olive oil
2 large Spanish onions, sliced
4 large tomatoes, sliced but not peeled
1 large fresh goat's cheese (300 g / 10 oz)
1 teaspoon thyme flowers
2 basil leaves, torn
2 garlic cloves, crushed

*Serves 6*

Preheat the oven to 220°C / 425°F / gas mark 7.

Sprinkle the aubergine slices with salt and lemon juice and set aside for 30 minutes.

Heat 2 tablespoons of the olive oil in a frying pan and sauté the aubergines on both sides until golden-brown. Sauté the onion slices until transparent, making sure they stay quite firm.

Oil an oblong earthenware baking dish. Arrange layers of aubergine slices, onions, tomatoes, and sliced cheese in the dish. Sprinkle the layers with the thyme flowers, basil and crushed garlic. Drizzle the top with the remaining olive oil.

Bake in the heated oven for 20 minutes. Serve warm, straight from the dish with an anchovy sauce.

## Sauce aux Anchois

ANCHOVY SAUCE

6 anchovy fillets
2 garlic cloves
1 teaspoon chopped flat-leaved parsley
3 basil leaves, torn
1 tablespoon lemon juice
4 tablespoons olive oil
pepper

Pound the anchovy fillets together with the garlic, parsley and basil. Add the lemon juice and mix well, then gradually whisk in the olive oil.

Serve in a sauce-boat with a fork or a miniature hand whisk so that the sauce can be whisked thoroughly before each helping for full flavour.

## Melon de Cavaillon au Beaume de Venise

FRENCH MELON WITH BEAUME DE VENISE

4 Charentais or Cavaillon melons
150 ml / 5 fl oz Beaume de Venise

*To decorate*
2 tablespoons redcurrants
a few mint leaves

*Serves 4*

Cut each melon crosswise at about two-thirds of their height. Discard the fibres and seeds. Carefully scoop out the flesh and cut it into small cubes or small round balls. Keep the shells in a cool place. Transfer the melon cubes or balls to a salad bowl. Pour over the wine and leave to macerate in a cool place for 1 hour. Before serving, spoon the fruit back into each melon. Decorate with currants and mint.

# Supper

## Soupe de Haricots Frais à la Tomate

FRESH HARICOT BEAN AND TOMATO SOUP

1 tablespoon olive oil
2 onions, chopped
1 kg / 2 lb tomatoes, peeled, seeded and quartered
3 garlic cloves, crushed
1 bouquet garni (thyme, bay leaf, celery leaf and savory)
1 litre / 1¾ pints chicken stock
salt and pepper
300 g / 10 oz fresh haricot beans, shelled
2 basil leaves, chopped
1 tablespoon chopped flat-leaved parsley

*Serves 4*

Heat the oil in a deep saucepan or flameproof casserole and soften the onion until transparent. Add the tomatoes, garlic and bouquet garni. Pour in the chicken stock. Season with pepper and bring to the boil. Add the beans and the basil. Reduce the heat, cover and simmer for 40 minutes. (If fresh haricot beans are not available, use dried: soak overnight, then drain before adding to the soup.) Add salt to taste and simmer for a further 5 minutes. Transfer the soup to a tureen, sprinkle with the parsley and serve at once.

## Gnocchi de Pommes de Terre au Pistou

BAKED POTATO CAKES WITH PESTO

*For the gnocchi*
1 kg / 2 lb large potatoes
50 g / 2 oz butter
100 g / 4 oz Gruyère or Emmental cheese, grated
1 teaspoon chopped chives
a pinch of freshly grated nutmeg
100 g / 4 oz strong white flour
salt and pepper

*For the pistou*
1 large garlic clove
6 basil leaves
1 teaspoon olive oil
50 g / 2 oz butter
1 large tomato, grilled
100 g / 4 oz Parmesan cheese, freshly grated

*Serves 4*

Preheat the oven to 190°C / 375°F / gas mark 5.

Wash the potatoes, dry them and prick them all over with a fork. Place them in the heated oven for 1 hour or until they are tender in the centre when tested with a thin skewer.

Halve the potatoes and scoop the flesh out into a mixing bowl. Add the butter, cheese, chives, nutmeg, salt and pepper to the potato mixture and mash together with a fork. Sift the flour over the potato purée and work in with a spatula.

Flour a wooden board. Scoop out dessert-spoonfuls of the mixture, sprinkle with flour and roll into small balls between the palms of the hands. Flatten each one gently with a fork into an even round. Chill for 30 minutes.

To cook the gnocchi: bring a large amount of salted water to the boil in a large saucepan. Lower 5–6 gnocchi into the water and poach for 10 minutes. Using a slotted spoon, transfer to a flat colander, then pat dry on kitchen paper. Cook the remainder in the same way. Arrange the gnocchi, overlapping, in a generously buttered gratin dish. Preheat the oven to 230°C / 450°F / gas mark 8.

To make the pistou: pound the garlic in a mortar with the basil, oil, butter and grilled tomato. Add the grated Parmesan cheese and mix well. Season with freshly ground black pepper.

Dot this mixture over each gnocchi and place in the heated oven for 10 minutes, then under a preheated grill for 2 minutes. Serve at once.

# Lunch

## Tatin de Tomates aux Herbes

UPSIDE-DOWN TOMATO TART

*For the demi-feuilletée pastry*
225 g / 8 oz strong white flour
a pinch of salt
100 g / 4 oz butter
125 ml / 4 fl oz iced water

*For the filling*
2 kg / 4 lb large firm tomatoes
4 tablespoons olive oil
1 heaped tablespoon soft brown sugar
1 stem of rosemary
1 garlic clove, finely chopped
4 basil leaves, torn
a sprinkling of fresh thyme
salt and pepper

*Serves 6*

To make the pastry: sift the flour with the salt on to a large wooden board. Cut the butter into small pieces and dot them all over the flour. Make a well in the centre and pour in the iced water. Working quickly with cool floured fingertips, work the butter into the flour, then draw the butter and flour into the water until a smooth dough is formed. Knead 2–3 times with the palms of the hands, shape into a ball and chill for 15 minutes.

Roll the dough out to an oblong about 1 cm / ½ inch thick. Turn the dough so that the short end is facing you. Fold the bottom third over towards the middle, then the top third over the folded third, just as you would fold a napkin. Chill for another 15 minutes. Return the dough to the board and repeat the rolling, folding and chilling another 3 times. Keep the pastry cool until ready.

Two or three hours before making the tart, prepare the filling. Leave the tomatoes for 5 minutes in a bowl filled with boiling water. Lift out, dry and peel each one. Then slice into thick, even slices.

Heat the oil, sugar and rosemary in a large heavy-based frying-pan. As soon as the mixture starts to caramelize, add the tomatoes, garlic, basil and thyme. Season and cook, uncovered, over a low heat for 30 minutes, stirring from time to time.

Transfer the tomatoes to a colander placed over a plate and leave to cool while the excess juices drip.

Preheat the oven to 220°C / 425°F / gas mark 7.

Grease the inside of a 30-cm / 12-inch deep non-stick flan tin with the excess oil which has dripped from the colander. Carefully spoon the tomato and herb mixture over the base.

Roll out the pastry to a round slightly larger than the tin. Cover the tomatoes with the pastry, pushing the sides towards the base of the tin. Bake for 20–25 minutes or until the pastry is puffed, crisp and golden-brown.

Take the tart out of the oven and turn it upside down on to a flat serving plate. Eat hot or lukewarm.

## *Gayettes Provençales aux Blettes*

SMALL PATTIES OF MINCED PORK AND SWISS CHARD

225 g / 8 oz Swiss chard leaves
225 g / 8 oz spinach
6 basil leaves
1 stem fresh thyme
1 teaspoon chopped flat-leaved parsley
1 teaspoon chopped celery leaves
1 tablespoon olive oil
50 g / 2 oz pig's liver, minced or very finely chopped
200 g / 7 oz minced belly of pork
a pinch of freshly ground nutmeg
50 g / 2 oz plain flour
1 sheet of caul fat (ask your butcher to prepare this)
a little butter, for greasing
sage leaves

*Serves 6*

Wash the chard and spinach and blanch them in boiling salted water for 3 minutes. Preheat the oven to 180°C / 350°F / gas mark 4.

Drain the greens and dry. Chop with the basil and mix with the thyme, parsley and celery leaves.

Heat the oil in a frying pan and quickly sauté the liver and minced pork. Season with salt, pepper and nutmeg. Leave to cool slightly, then transfer to a mixing bowl and work in the flour, greens and herbs.

Soak the caul fat in a small amount of tepid water. Divide it into 12.5-cm / 5-inch squares.

Divide the meat and vegetable mixture into round patties. Lay one of the caul fat squares over one hand, put a ball of the mixture in the centre and wrap it up.

Grease an earthenware baking dish. Lay the *gayettes* in the dish. Put a sage leaf on each one. Pour water into the dish and bake for 40 minutes until the top is browned. Eat hot or cold, with a green salad.

*Once lightly grilled, the figs will be served in an antique Moustier dish and eaten with walnut bread*

## *Pain aux Noix*

WALNUT BREAD

20 g / ¾ oz fresh yeast
¼ teaspoon sugar
350 ml / 12 fl oz warm water
1 tablespoon clear honey
2 teaspoons salt
750 g / 1½ lb plain wholemeal flour
100 g / 4 oz shelled walnuts, coarsely chopped

Place the yeast and sugar in a small bowl, add 2 tablespoons of the water and mash until smooth. Set aside until the mixture is frothy and increased in volume.

Meanwhile mix the honey with the remaining water and salt.

Sift the flour into a large mixing bowl and make a well in the centre. Pour the yeast and water and honey and water mixtures into the well and mix together. Dot the walnuts all over the flour and, using your fingertips, draw the flour and walnuts into the liquid.

When the dough is well mixed and coming away from the sides of the bowl, turn it out on to a lightly floured work surface and knead well for 10–15 minutes or until the dough is smooth.

Rinse out the mixing bowl and grease it lightly. Shape the dough into a ball and place in the bowl. Cover with a clean damp cloth and set aside in a warm room for 1 hour or until the dough has doubled in size.

Turn the dough on to a work surface and punch it to knock out the air. Knead it for about 5 minutes, then transfer it to a greased 1-kg / 2-lb loaf tin. Set aside until the dough has doubled in size again. Meanwhile preheat the oven to 220°C / 425°F / gas mark 7. Bake the loaf for 40–45 minutes or until it is puffed up, crusty and brown. Serve warm.

## *Figues Confites au Chèvre Frais*

BAKED FRESH FIGS WITH FRESH GOAT'S CHEESE

12 fresh figs
1 tablespoon clear honey
1 tablespoon melted butter
a pinch of summer savory
freshly ground black pepper
2 small fresh goat's cheeses

*Serves 6*

Preheat the grill.

Cut the figs lengthways and open out without detaching the bottom. Mix the honey with the melted butter and the summer savory. Using a pastry brush, brush the flesh of the figs with the honey mixture. Season with black pepper. Place the figs under the heated grill for a few minutes until they start to caramelize. Slide a thin slice of goat's cheese inside each fig and leave to melt for 2–3 minutes. Eat warm with walnut bread.

# The Cherry Orchard

The elegant pink house is set in a cherry orchard facing the river Seine. We are near Villequier, the native village of Victor Hugo, in a valley planted with cherry orchards years back, by the monks of the nearby abbey of Jumièges.

The trees are heavy with fruit. Friends and family have been called in by the Gauthiers to help with the picking.

It is all such fun. While the younger generation climb up the ladders filling baskets by the minute, little girls hang the shiny crimson fruit around their ears or on their straw hats. In the huge kitchen the perfume of fruit is unbelievable. Aunts and *grand'-mères* are busy making jam, sterilizing, bottling or pickling the less ripe fruit in spiced vinegar. I am in charge of luncheon. The oven is the only cooking facility available, so we will have *papillottes* of chicken. The first course, a terrine of young leeks, was prepared yesterday, as well as the cherry dessert, the indispensable final course of our cherry feast.

For the evening meal I have made a chicken broth with a boiling fowl. A few young vegetables added to the broth will make a light summer soup. With the cooked hen, I shall prepare a *mousseline de volaille* – a light chicken mousse that I serve with a strong cream and leek sauce. We will finish with a warm *compote* of rhubarb and spiced cherries flamed with kirsch.

*Preserves from the cherry orchard*

*The leek terrine*

LUNCH

## *Terrine de Poireaux à la Gribiche de Cerfeuil*

LEEK TERRINE WITH A CHOPPED EGG AND HERB DRESSING

3 kg / 5½ lb small young leeks
salt and pepper

*For the dressing*
2 tablespoons leek stock
2 hard-boiled eggs
1 tablespoon finely chopped chives
4 nasturtium leaves, finely chopped
2 tablespoons chopped chervil
6 tablespoons grapeseed oil
2 tablespoons walnut oil
2 tablespoons sherry vinegar

*To decorate*
6 nasturtium flowers, 12 nasturtium leaves
or chopped chervil or parsley

*Serves 6*

Line a 1-kg / 2-lb ovenproof glass or terrine dish or loaf tin with kitchen foil, leaving some foil overlapping the edges of the tin.

Wash the leeks carefully under cold running water, discard the toughest leaves and trim them to the same length as the base of the tin. Bring a large saucepan of salted water to the boil and cook the leeks for 10 minutes or until just tender. Keep some of the cooking liquid for the sauce.

Immediately transfer the leeks to a colander and run under a cold tap. Leave to drain for a while, pressing down from time to time to make sure all the cooking liquid has been extracted.

Place a layer of leeks at the base of the dish or tin with all the white parts at the same end. Season with salt and pepper. Cover with another layer, this time with the white at the other end, and so on until the dish or tin is full. Fold the foil over the top and press down with a weight. Leave until cold, then refrigerate for 12 hours.

To serve: turn the tin upside down on to a board and let the excess cooking liquid run out. Remove the foil, slice the terrine and transfer each slice to an individual plate.

Prepare the sauce: bring the leek stock to the boil. Finely chop the hard-boiled eggs and mix with the chives, nasturtium leaves and chervil. Make a vinaigrette dressing with the two oils and vinegar; combine with the egg and herbs and gradually whisk in 2 tablespoons of the leek stock.

Spoon the herb dressing over the leek terrine and decorate the dish with either the nasturtium flowers and leaves or the chopped chervil or parsley.

## *Papillotte de Poulet aux Pommes*

CHICKEN AND APPLE PARCELS

1 free-range chicken
3 tablespoons sunflower oil
4 crisp fragrant dessert apples
salt and pepper
1 teaspoon chopped thyme
4 sage leaves
2 tablespoons crème fraîche
125 ml / 4 fl oz Calvados
50 g / 2 oz butter

*Serves 4*

Cut the chicken into quarters. Heat the oil in a large frying-pan and seal the chicken pieces on all sides until they are golden-brown.

Preheat the oven to 190°C / 375°F / gas mark 5.

Peel the apples, leaving them whole. Core the centres with an apple corer and slice the apples crosswise into even round slices. Lightly oil 4 squares of kitchen foil. Place a chicken quarter at the centre of each square and sprinkle with salt, pepper and a touch of thyme. Place a sage leaf on top of each chicken quarter, then lay the apple slices over the chicken so that they overlap. Spoon a little crème fraîche and Calvados into the cavity of each apple slice. Dot with small pieces of butter. Fold the foil over and pleat the edges to seal.

Lay the *papillottes* on a baking tray and bake in the heated oven for 30–40 minutes according to the size of the chicken pieces.

Serve the *papillottes* at once, opening them up delicately, or carefully spoon out on to a serving plate.

*Later on in the season, cherries will give way to ripe apples*

## *Croquant de Cerises en Bavarois*

CHERRIES IN A CRISP ALMOND SHELL

*For the biscuit base*
200 g / 7 oz blanched almonds
75 g / 3 oz icing sugar
a pinch of salt
3 egg whites
15 g / ½ oz cornflour
butter, for greasing

*For the filling*
40 g / 1½ oz unsalted butter
175 g / 6 oz granulated sugar
750 g / 1½ lb cherries, stoned
2 tablespoons kirsch
150 g / 5 oz fromage blanc
8 g / ¼ oz powdered gelatine
100 g / 4 oz crème fraîche
⅓ teaspoon finely grated lemon zest

*Serves 6*

Preheat the oven to 200°C / 400°F / gas mark 6.

Prepare the base: grind the almonds in a blender until their consistency is at a stage between chopped and ground almonds. Mix them with the icing sugar. Add the salt to the egg whites in a deep bowl and whisk them until very stiff. Delicately fold in the almond–sugar mixture, then the cornflour. Chill for at least 30 minutes or until the mixture is firm.

Generously butter a disc of greaseproof paper to fit the base of a tart tin with removable sides. Place the buttered paper in the tin. Spread the almond mixture over the paper and smooth the surface evenly with a spatula.

Bake in the heated oven for 20 minutes or until the biscuit is golden and crisp. Leave to cool while you prepare the filling.

Melt the butter in a frying-pan with 50 g / 2 oz of the sugar. Add the cherries and sauté over a high heat, stirring well for 5 minutes. Add the kirsch, lower the heat and cook, stirring, for a further 10 minutes. Remove the fruit with a slotted spoon and set aside.

Sprinkle 75 g / 3 oz of the remaining sugar over the pan juices and reduce until the buttery juice starts to caramelize. Remove the pan from the heat. Roll the cherries in the flavoured caramel and leave to cool in the pan, shaking it from time to time.

Meanwhile, warm up 1 tablespoon of fromage blanc and dissolve the gelatine in it. Using a hand whisk, whisk the gelatine into the remaining fromage blanc, then whisk in the remaining sugar and the lemon zest. Whisk the cream until quite firm and fold it into the fromage blanc. Pour the creamy mixture over the biscuit base in the tin. Refrigerate for 2 hours.

To serve: remove the outer ring and slide the dessert on to a flat serving platter. Separate the caramelized cherries, arrange them closely over the top of the tart and serve.

*The cherry orchard*

*Near Duclair, the indigenous cherry tart*

## DINNER

### Potage de Fèves à la Julienne Printanière

BROAD BEAN AND YOUNG VEGETABLE BROTH

225 g / 8 oz shelled broad beans
2 large tomatoes
10 small new carrots
6 baby turnips
1 bunch of radishes
6 young leeks
1 stick of celery
2 small courgettes
1.5 litres / 2½ pints well-flavoured chicken stock
1 teaspoon chopped chervil
1 teaspoon chopped chives
1 teaspoon chopped summer savory
50 g / 2 oz butter

*Serves 6–8*

Blanch the broad beans in boiling salted water for 5 minutes. Transfer to a colander and place under cold running water for a few seconds. Peel off the outer skin of each bean.

Blanch the tomatoes and peel them. Cut them into quarters and squeeze out the seeds. Wash and peel the other vegetables and slice them downwards and across into thin oblong pieces.

Bring the chicken stock to the boil in a large saucepan. Add the julienne of vegetables and the broad beans to the stock and boil for 8 minutes. The vegetables should stay slightly crisp.

Mash the mixed herbs into the butter. Whisk the butter mixture into the soup and serve in a tureen.

### Mousseline de Volaille à la Crème de Poireau

CHICKEN LEEK WITH CREAMY LEEK SAUCE

500 g / 1 lb cooked chicken breast, cold
3 egg whites
4 egg yolks
200 g / 7 oz crème fraîche
salt and pepper
a pinch of freshly grated nutmeg
2 teaspoons tomato purée
a pinch of chopped tarragon

*For the dish*
25 g / 1 oz butter
1 tablespoon cornflour

*For the sauce*
500 g / 1 lb young leeks
75 g / 3 oz butter
250 ml / 8 fl oz crème fraîche
salt and pepper

*Serves 4*

Preheat the oven to 180°C / 350°F / gas mark 4.

Mince the chicken through a food mill into a large mixing bowl. Add 2 of the egg whites and mix well with a spatula. Work in the egg yolks, one by one, then the crème fraîche. Mix well. Season with salt and pepper, the nutmeg, tomato purée and tarragon.

Grease the inside of a 1-litre / 2-pint soufflé dish with butter. Sprinkle the cornflour over the base and sides and tap off the excess.

Whisk the remaining egg white until stiff and fold into the chicken mixture.

Turn the chicken mixture into the soufflé dish. Stand it in a bain-marie of warm water and bake in the heated oven for 30–35 minutes or until well risen and firm to the touch.

Meanwhile, prepare the sauce: trim the leeks, keeping as much green as possible. Wash the leeks carefully under cold running water and slice them downwards and across into oblong pieces. Place the butter in a saucepan, cover with the leeks and leave to sweat over a low heat, stirring from time to time, until they are tender. Make sure they do not brown at all; if necessary add a little water. Purée the leeks to a smooth paste in a blender.

Return the purée to the pan. Now add the crème fraîche and season with freshly ground salt and pepper. Warm through slowly, stirring constantly, until the sauce thickens.

To serve: allow the chicken *mousseline* to cool slightly, then turn out on to a heated serving platter. Spoon some of the hot leek sauce around the *mousseline* and serve the rest in a sauce-boat.

## Compote de Rhubarbe aux Cerises Épicées

RHUBARB AND SPICED CHERRY COMPOTE

500 g / 1 lb rhubarb
200 g / 7 oz caster sugar
1 kg / 2 lb cherries
1 cinnamon stick
1 vanilla pod, halved
1 teaspoon finely grated orange rind
1 teaspoon finely grated lemon rind
150 g / 5 oz chopped pistachios
4 tablespoons kirsch

*Serves 6*

Trim the rhubarb and cut it into small regular pieces. Transfer the fruit to a mixing bowl and sprinkle with 50 g / 2 oz of the sugar.

Leave in a cool place for 1 hour to draw out the bitter juices, then drain. Turn the rhubarb into a pan and cook it with 50 g / 2 oz more sugar and a dessertspoon of water for 10 minutes or until just tender.

Stone the cherries and poach them with the remaining sugar and the spices, reserving the pistachios for the decoration.

To serve: remove the cinnamon stick and the vanilla pod. Mix the cherries and rhubarb and leave to cool until lukewarm. Sprinkle the pistachios over the top of the *compote*. Warm the kirsch in a small saucepan, set light and pour it while still flaming over the fruit. Serve at once.

*Baskets ready for the gathering of cherries*

# The Nostalgic Garden

*Grand'-mère's redcurrant tart*

My cousin Huguette lives near Cognac in a house which used to belong to our grandmother.

'Have you still got the recipe Grand'-mère used to make with the first redcurrants?' I asked when I telephoned to invite myself.

'Come straight down. I make the tart every year and the currants are just ripe,' answered my cousin.

*Childhood nostalgia*

*Woodland flowers*

Huguette has preserved the house of our youth perfectly: the old lady's chair, the clock and the pretty blue glasses in which, even as children, we were allowed to sip raspberry wine or a drop of home-made *crème de cassis.*

The garden has not changed either. Lilac, flowering currants, the camellia and the warped gravel path bordered by a box hedge which hides soft fruit and vegetables. And then, pecking away in their trellised corner, hens, pigeons, a goose and a few ducks.

Our grandmother used to consider vegetables unsightly, hence the box hedge. As a child, I loved to bruise the box's leaves between my fingers; their incense aroma reminded me of church. There was no need to go to Mass; my own little place of worship was at the bottom of that garden.

Today, a light meal has been prepared with garden produce from recipes that our dear *Grand'-mère* would not have dreamed of making. Yet the *terrine de légumes* followed by a chicken baked in a coarse sea-salt crust have left enough room to allow the tangy tart, without a word, but just an exchange of looks, to bring back the happy past of childhood holidays.

## Lunch

## *Terrine de Légumes d'Été au Coulis de Tomate*

SUMMER VEGETABLE TERRINE WITH FRESH TOMATO SAUCE

*For the terrine*

2 red peppers
4 courgettes
4 large tomatoes
olive oil
6 small spring onions, chopped
3 fresh garlic cloves, crushed
8 eggs, beaten
2 teaspoons chopped chives
1 teaspoon chopped parsley
3 basil leaves, chopped
salt and pepper
a pinch of freshly grated nutmeg

*For the sauce*

500 g / 1 lb ripe tomatoes, peeled and chopped
2 small garlic cloves, crushed
4 tablespoons olive oil
2 teaspoons lemon juice
4 basil leaves, chopped

*Serves 4–6*

Preheat the oven to 200°C / 400°F / gas mark 6.

To prepare the terrine: dice the peppers, courgettes and tomatoes. Heat some oil in a frying-pan and sauté the prepared vegetables with the spring onions until tender. Lower the heat if necessary; none of the vegetables must be allowed to brown. Add the garlic, mix well and sauté for a further 5 minutes.

Meanwhile, line the inside of an ovenproof glass or china terrine dish with oiled greaseproof paper. Take the pan containing the vegetables off the heat, allow to cool slightly, then stir in the beaten eggs, herbs, salt, pepper and nutmeg. Pour immediately into the terrine dish. Cover loosely with kitchen foil. Stand the dish in a bain-marie of warm water and bake in the heated oven for 45 minutes.

Meanwhile, prepare the sauce: blend all the ingredients briefly in a liquidizer. Chill.

When the terrine is set, remove from the oven and leave to cool in the tin. Turn out on to a serving platter and chill. Serve with the tomato *coulis*.

## Poulet aux Herbes en Croûte de Sel

CHICKEN BAKED INSIDE A COARSE SEA-SALT CRUST

1 teaspoon chopped thyme
1 teaspoon chopped tarragon
1 teaspoon chopped parsley
a few coriander leaves
2 tablespoons olive oil
freshly ground black pepper
1 free-range chicken (1.5 kg / 3 lb)
1 lemon

*For the sea-salt crust*
1 kg / 2 lb strong white flour
1 kg / 2 lb coarse sea salt
iced water

*Serves 4*

The day before, mix all the herbs with the olive oil and freshly ground black pepper. Rub the chicken inside and outside with the mixture. Cover loosely and refrigerate.

Preheat the oven to 200°C / 400°F / gas mark 6.

To prepare the sea-salt crust: sift the flour into a large mixing bowl. Draw in the sea salt and water. Mix well with fingertips and knead to a rough dough.

Cut the dough in half. Roll out one half on a large wooden board. Place the chicken in the centre.

Roll out the remaining dough and wrap the chicken totally, making sure that the dough is of a consistent thickness all round and that no air can get to the fowl.

Bake in the heated oven for 1½ hours. To serve: break the crust and carve the chicken on a heated serving platter. Mix the cooking juices with a little lemon juice, check the seasoning and spoon juices over the meat.

*Box hedging around fruit and vegetable beds*

## Tarte Meringuée aux Groseilles

REDCURRANT MERINGUE TART

*For the pastry*
200 g / 7 oz plain flour
a pinch of salt
100 g / 4 oz caster sugar
100 g / 4 oz unsalted butter
2 eggs, beaten

*For the filling*
100 g / 4 oz flaked almonds
½ teaspoon finely grated lemon zest
2 tablespoons redcurrant jelly
100 g / 4 oz ground almonds
200 g / 7 oz caster sugar
500 g / 1 lb redcurrants
5 egg whites
1 tablespoon icing sugar

*Serves 4–6*

To make the pastry: sift the flour, salt and sugar on to a large wooden board. Cut the butter into small pieces and dot them over the flour. With cool floured fingertips, working quickly, rub the butter into the flour. Make a well in the centre and pour in the eggs. Draw in the eggs until a smooth dough has been obtained. Knead 2–3 times with the palms of the hands. Shape into a ball, cover with clingfilm and chill for 30 minutes before rolling out.

Preheat the oven to 200°C / 400°F / gas mark 6.

Roll out the pastry to line a 30-cm / 12-inch tart dish. Cover the pastry with foil and baking beans and bake blind in the heated oven for 15 minutes. Remove the beans and bake for a further 5 minutes. Remove from the oven and leave to cool.

Meanwhile, toast the almonds in a non-stick frying-pan. Fold them, with the lemon zest, into the redcurrant jelly and spread over the pastry case.

*French statue in the garden*

Sift the ground almonds with 100 g / 4 oz of the sugar into a bowl. Carefully strip the currants off their stems into the same bowl and gently coat the currants with the sweetened ground almonds, using your fingers.

Reduce the oven heat to 180°C / 350°F / gas mark 4.

Whisk the egg whites until stiff. Sift the remaining sugar with the icing sugar and gradually add it to the whites as they start to firm up. Gently fold in the redcurrants.

Spoon the mixture into the pastry case and bake for 40–50 minutes or until the meringue is crisp and golden-brown.

*The dovecote*

# A Nineteenth-Century Potager

At the Domaine du Closel, in Savennières, a charming village in the Loire Valley, Madame de Jessey keeps a commanding eye on acres of vines and the production of her excellent *appellation contrôlée* white wine. At the same time, she runs with great charm a large house filled with children and grandchildren throughout the summer. She also finds time personally to tend the huge nineteenth-century *potager*, in the style of Gabriel Thonin, the leading French landscape architect of that period. It is big enough to feed the family, the cook and other staff.

The *potager* backs on to the church and the village square and runs down to watermeadows and a natural lake. The layout is typical of the period, in the form of four huge squares which form an arbour for the four seasons' vegetables and soft fruit. At the centre stands a large well surrounded by fruit trees. Lettuces are grown under antique glass cloches, whilst melons and Chasselas grapes cluster in long curviform glasshouses. The only exotic touch is the kiwi plant which clambers over the south-facing wall.

Madame de Jessey very kindly allowed me the run of the kitchen and I prepared a cream of artichoke heart soup with chervil, to be followed by a guinea-fowl laced with the Domaine's wine and grapes. To finish, a buttery apple and quince tart baked with a hint of cinnamon.

*Reading all the strawberry recipes*

## LUNCH

### *Velouté de Fonds d'Artichaut au Cerfeuil*

CREAM OF ARTICHOKE HEART SOUP WITH CHERVIL

6 artichokes
salt and pepper
750 ml / 1¼ pints chicken stock
1 tablespoon milk
2 teaspoons cornflour
125 ml / 4 fl oz crème fraîche
1 heaped tablespoon finely chopped chervil

*Serves 6*

Cut off the stalks at the base of the artichokes. Cook for 45 minutes in plenty of salted boiling water. Drain well, heads down, in a colander. When the artichokes are cool enough to handle, remove the outer leaves and the hairy chokes.

Place the artichoke hearts in a saucepan with the stock. Bring to the boil, then purée in a blender. Return the soup to the pan. Make a paste with the milk and cornflour. Stir gently into the soup until it thickens. Add the crème fraîche and chervil. Season to taste with salt and pepper. Stir for a few more minutes and serve at once.

*Plump artichokes and broccoli in the farm kitchen*

### *Pintade Vigneronne*

GUINEA-FOWL WITH GRAPES

225 g / 8 oz large seedless grapes
1 tablespoon Cognac
100 g / 4 oz butter
2 teaspoons grapeseed oil
100 g / 4 oz smoked bacon, cubed into lardons
2 shallots
1 guinea-fowl (1.5 kg / 3 lb)
2 garlic cloves, unpeeled
1 stem rosemary
1 sage leaf
salt and pepper
100 ml / 4 fl oz dry white wine
50 g / 2 oz pine nuts

*Serves 6*

Peel the grapes and soak in Cognac for 2 hours.

Preheat the oven to 200°C / 400°F / gas mark 6.

Heat half the butter with the oil in a flameproof casserole. Brown the lardons and shallots, remove and set aside. Seal the guinea-fowl on all sides until golden-brown, then transfer to a plate. Pour off all but 1 tablespoon of fat from the casserole.

Return the guinea-fowl to the casserole with the lardons, shallots, garlic, rosemary and sage leaf. Dot the remaining butter over the breast of the bird. Season with salt and pepper and add the wine. Cover, place the casserole in the heated oven and cook for 1 hour, or until the guinea-fowl is cooked through and tender.

Sauté the pine nuts in a non-stick frying-pan until golden-brown. Transfer the guinea-fowl to a heated platter and keep warm.

To make the sauce: discard the rosemary and sage leaf. Add the grapes and Cognac to the casserole, with a little warm water, and stir well to dissolve the cooking juices. Add the pine nuts and cook, uncovered, for a few minutes. Carve the guinea-fowl and spoon the sauce over the meat.

## *Tarte aux Pommes et aux Coings*

APPLE AND QUINCE TART

*For the pastry*
225 g / 8 oz plain flour
a pinch of salt
25 g / 1 oz caster sugar
100 g / 4 oz unsalted butter
1 egg
a little iced water

*For the filling*
2 large quinces
300 g / 10 oz soft brown sugar
1 vanilla pod, halved
2 large dessert apples
50 g / 2 oz flaked almonds
a pinch of ground cinnamon
40 g / 1½ oz unsalted butter

*Serves 6*

To make the pastry: sift the flour with the salt and sugar on to a large wooden board. Dot with the butter, cut into small pieces. Make a well in the centre and add the egg. With cool floured fingertips, working quickly, rub the butter into the flour and then draw in the egg, adding a little iced water if necessary, until a smooth dough has been obtained. Knead 2–3 times with the palms of the hands. Shape into a ball and leave to rest, covered, for 30 minutes before rolling out.

Meanwhile, peel and core the quinces. Tie the peel up in a piece of muslin and core and divide the fruit into quarters. Place the quince and peel in a saucepan, cover with water and add 250 g / 9 oz of the sugar and the vanilla pod. Poach the quince for 25 minutes or until tender. Remove the fruit with a slotted spoon and set aside to cool. Bring the cooking juices to the boil and reduce over a medium heat until almost completely reduced, thick and syrupy.

Preheat the oven to 200°C / 400°F / gas mark 6.

Peel the apples and cut them into thin, even slices. Slice the poached quince.

Roll out the pastry to line a 30-cm / 12-inch tart dish. Sprinkle the almonds over the pastry.

Alternate the fruit over the almonds in a circular pattern. Sift the cinnamon with the remaining sugar and sprinkle over the fruit. Dot with the butter and bake in the heated oven for 30–35 minutes. When the tart is cooked, glaze the fruit with the reduced quince syrup. Allow to cool and serve on its own or with lightly whipped cream.

# *The Tidy Garden*

Séverine and André both work in the Norman city of Rouen and live just on the outskirts, in a house typical of the region, made of stone and brickwork with brown shutters and trailing geraniums on each window-sill.

There is a small square lawn with an apple tree and most of the flowers are grown either against the house or in large pots judiciously placed on the gravel path which surrounds the house. The rest of the flat garden is devoted to vegetables.

This garden is Séverine and André's passion, and they keep it meticulously, in impeccable straight rows, without a single weed. A perfect example of French tidiness? Maybe, but such a charming one, for it reminds one of the early domestic vegetable gardens laid out for practicality, like a miniature market gardener's world. Even the empty packets of seeds have been pinched between wooden sticks at the end of each row, as a reminder of the name and the variety of each plant. The choice is classic: every species is there. It is an orderly garden designed to feed the family all year round.

I have been invited for Sunday lunch and dinner. The lunch-time meal is classically gargantuan. We start with a creamy spinach tart, followed by a splendid duck braised in a heavy red wine sauce and served with small stuffed cabbage parcels; then there is some lettuce in a

*Carrots in a basket*

chive and shallot dressing, then cheese and finally a light gratin of blackberries.

Dinner will be very light, I am told. A delicious soup served steaming in a huge tureen and then, after cheese, of course, some wonderful baked apples on a bed of sweet brioche served with a tangy cider sauce. *Quelle* feast! May I come every Sunday? I'll gladly help with the weeding.

## Lunch

### *Tarte aux Épinards Normande*

CREAMY SPINACH TART

300 g / 10 oz *pâte demi-feuilletée* (see page 94)
750 g / 1½ lb fresh spinach
50 g / 2 oz butter
2 eggs
2 tablespoons crème fraîche
225 g / 8 oz fromage blanc
50 g / 2 oz Parmesan cheese, freshly grated
freshly grated nutmeg
salt and pepper

*Serves 6*

Preheat the oven to 200°C / 400°F / gas mark 6.

Put a baking sheet in the oven to heat. Line a 30-cm / 12-inch tart tin with the pastry, cover with foil and baking beans and bake blind on the hot baking sheet for about 15 minutes, until the pastry has started to set. Remove from the oven, remove the foil and beans and leave to cool.

Wash the spinach under cold running water and pat dry with kitchen paper. Place the butter and spinach in a saucepan and sweat over a low heat, stirring from time to time, for about 8–10 minutes. Remove from the heat and leave to cool slightly.

Meanwhile, beat the eggs with the crème fraîche and the fromage blanc. Add the Parmesan cheese, salt, pepper and nutmeg. Make sure the spinach is completely dry, then add it to the fromage blanc and egg mixture. Mix well and check the seasoning. Spoon the mixture over the pastry case and bake in the heated oven for 20 minutes or until the filling is set and golden on top.

### *Daube de Canard Rouennaise aux Farcis de Chou*

DUCK BRAISED IN RED WINE WITH SMALL CABBAGE PARCELS

1 farm duck
2 teaspoons sea salt
4 shallots, chopped
1 teaspoon brandy
300 ml / 10 fl oz good red wine
1 sage leaf
1 bouquet garni (parsley, thyme, bay leaf)
black pepper

*For the vegetables*
6 large cabbage leaves
3 carrots, peeled
2 turnips
1 stick celery
15 g / ½ oz butter
100 g / 4 oz smoked bacon, cubed into lardons
1 shallot, chopped
225 g / 8 oz shelled peas

*For the* beurre manié
25 g / 1 oz butter
1 teaspoon plain flour

*Serves 6*

Preheat the oven to 230°C / 450°F / gas mark 8.

Clean and truss the duck, cut off the gland on top of the parson's nose to avoid too strong a taste, prick the skin all over and rub with sea salt. Put the duck into a roasting pan and brown it in the oven until the fat beneath the skin has melted. This will take about 30–40 minutes. During that time, reduce the oven heat if necessary. Remove the duck from the oven and set aside.

Heat 1 tablespoon of the duck fat in a flameproof casserole and sauté the shallots until transparent. Place the duck on the bed of shallots in the casserole, add the brandy, red wine, sage leaf and bouquet garni. Season with freshly ground black pepper. Cover, reduce the heat and simmer for 50–60 minutes or until tender.

Meanwhile, prepare the vegetables. Blanch the cabbage leaves for 5 minutes in salted boiling water. Run under the cold tap, drain well and pat dry thoroughly between sheets of kitchen paper. Chop the carrots, turnips and celery into very small cubes and blanch in salted boiling water for approximately 8–10 minutes.

Heat the butter in a frying-pan and sauté the bacon lardons and shallots together until the shallots are limp and transparent. Drain the other vegetables and transfer them to the frying-pan with the lardons, shallots and peas. Cover and reduce the heat to simmering point. Simmer for 6 minutes.

Place the cabbage leaves vein side up on a work surface. Spoon some of the vegetable and bacon mixture on to the centre of each leaf. Fold the edges inwards and roll up the leaf from the stem end to form a neat parcel. Secure with a small wooden skewer. Transfer the cabbage parcels to a steamer, metal colander or large sieve and keep warm over boiling water.

To finish preparing the duck: transfer the duck from the casserole to a heated platter and keep warm in a low oven while making the sauce.

Skim the excess fat from the cooking liquid. Discard the bouquet garni and sage leaf. Bring the sauce to the boil, scraping up all the cooking juices and adding a little water if the sauce is too short. Strain the sauce into a saucepan.

Make the *beurre manié*: mash the flour into the butter. Divide into small pieces. Warm the sauce and whisk in the *beurre manié*, piece by piece, stirring well until the sauce is very smooth. Check the seasoning.

Carve the duck on to a serving platter. Spoon the sauce over the duck pieces. Serve with the cabbage parcels arranged around the meat.

*Watering the garden the old-fashioned way*

## *Gratin de Mûres*

GRATIN OF BLACKBERRIES

500 g / 1 lb blackberries
100 g / 4 oz caster sugar
3 egg yolks
3 tablespoons double cream
½ teaspoon finely grated lemon zest

*Serves 6*

Preheat the oven to 230°C / 450°F / gas mark 8.

Carefully wash the blackberries and pat them dry with kitchen paper. Divide the fruit among 6 individual ovenproof baking dishes.

Cream the sugar and egg yolks in a mixing bowl until light and frothy. Lightly whip the double cream and fold it into the egg and sugar mixture. Add the lemon zest. Pour the mixture over the fruit and bake in the heated oven for 8–10 minutes or until the cream starts bubbling and becomes golden-brown. Serve at once.

# Dinner

## *Velouté Maraîcher à la Chiffonnade d'Oseille*

SPRING VEGETABLE SOUP WITH SORREL

300 g / 10 oz young leeks
4 spring onions
50 g / 2 oz butter
750 ml / 1¼ pints chicken stock
225 g / 8 oz potatoes, diced
225 g / 8 oz shelled peas
2 teaspoons cornflour
1 tablespoon milk
1 tablespoon crème fraîche
1 small lettuce heart
6 sorrel leaves
a handful of chervil
salt and pepper

*Serves 6*

*Blackberries baked with a frothy topping*

Trim the leeks and discard the toughest green leaves, leaving as much tender green as possible. Wash the leeks carefully under cold running water and slice them downwards and across into oblong pieces. Peel and thinly slice the spring onions. Place the butter in a large saucepan, cover with the leeks and onions and leave the vegetables to sweat over a low heat for a few minutes. Then pour in the chicken stock.

Add the potatoes and peas and cook over a medium heat for 15–20 minutes or until the vegetables are tender.

Purée all the vegetables in a blender and return the soup to the pan. Make a paste with the cornflour and milk and stir gently into the soup until it thickens. Add the crème fraîche.

Wash and finely shred the lettuce heart, sorrel and chervil. Add them to the soup, stir well and leave to infuse for a few minutes. Serve in a soup tureen.

*Fermenting apples*

## Pommes Cuites au Beurre de Cidre

BAKED APPLES IN A CIDER SAUCE

6 dessert apples
juice of 1 lemon
6 teaspoons soft brown sugar
50 g / 2 oz unsalted butter
6 round slices of brioche

*For the cider sauce*
a 75-cl bottle sweet cider
1 tablespoon clear honey
1 teaspoon Calvados
100 g / 4 oz unsalted butter
1 tablespoon crème fraîche

*Serves 6*

Preheat the oven to 200°C / 400°F / gas mark 6.

Peel and core the apples. Arrange them in a large saucepan, cover them with boiling water and the lemon juice and blanch for 5 minutes. Drain the fruit well and pat dry.

Arrange the brioche slices in a large earthenware baking dish. Place an apple on each one. Sprinkle the apples with sugar and dot with the butter. Bake in the heated oven for 15–20 minutes or until the apples are tender but not mushy.

Towards the end of cooking time make the cider butter sauce.

In a saucepan, boil the cider and honey until reduced to one-fifth. Add the Calvados. Cut the butter into small pieces and whisk into the liquid until the sauce has thickened and is frothy. Stir in the crème fraîche.

To serve: spoon the sauce on to individual plates. Place the baked apple and brioche in the centre of each plate and serve hot.

# An Exceptional Potager

Huge parkland stretches out in all directions around Tournelay, a large château set alongside the river Argent by the village of Nueil-sur-Argent, in the Deux-Sèvres, a sleepy region in central France.

The property belongs to General and Baronne Gérard de Lassus and is an exceptionally well-preserved example of a French nineteenth-century estate. Over 200 traditional French trees, young and old, grow in this botanic paradise. Well-kept paths lead to an old lake, a cascade, a wood and a remarkable *potager* with a pheasant and pigeon aviary at its entrance, as well as the original hen-house filled with a myriad birds.

I retain fond memories of this visit, for I was met and given a guided tour by the General and Baronne's fourteen grandchildren, aged between three and eleven. The little girls all wore the same pretty cotton dresses. One of them took me aside and revealed that she understood very well why I could be so interested by such a beautiful *potager* but 'Did we need to go as far as taking pictures of courgettes?'

We joyously visited the orderly kitchen garden. Originally designed to feed the forty people who lived and worked on the estate, the *potager* is walled on all sides to protect plants, flowers and fruit trees from the wind. In the middle there is a pond, and grapes are grown in antique glasshouses

*Huge parkland surrounds the château*

*Courgettes and tomatoes: ideal for light summer dishes*

whilst the pears, grown *en espalier,* are each wrapped in a small bag to protect them from the bees and insects. Every possible kind of French leguminous species grows here and there is also a large medicinal herb garden.

The Baronne gave me a simple but delicious family dessert recipe of apple and prunes baked in a charlotte dish which she serves either with whipped cream or *crème anglaise,* French home-made custard. She told me that she prepares many soups, some substantial goose and vegetable *garbures* from her native Périgord, and has a simple recipe for spaghetti with courgettes which seems to regale her grandchildren.

She very kindly let me choose a few vegetables from the garden and, in the kitchen with pretty gingham material on the tables and windows, I made a *mousseline de céléri-rave*, a light celeriac mousse which I served with a carrot butter. We followed this first course with home-reared guinea-fowl served with braised lettuce hearts, and finally the light apple and prune dessert. The children opted for the courgettes and spaghetti but the family dessert was shared by us all.

## Lunch

## *Mousseline de Céléri-rave au Beurre de Carottes*

CELERIAC MOUSSE WITH WARM CARROT BUTTER

*For the mousse*

600 g / 1¼ lb celeriac
juice of ½ lemon
salt and pepper
3 eggs
150 ml / 5 fl oz crème fraîche

*For the dishes*

25 g / 1 oz butter
2 teaspoons cornflour

*For the carrot butter*

225 g / 8 oz carrots
100 g / 4 oz butter
3 teaspoons finely chopped chives
salt and pepper

*Serves 6*

Peel and dice the celeriac. Immediately put the pieces into a bowl of water with the lemon juice added, so that they stay white. Bring a saucepan of salted water to the boil and then boil the celeriac for 15–20 minutes or until tender. Drain well and pat dry with kitchen paper, then purée in a food mill or blender.

Preheat the oven to 180°C / 350°F / gas mark 4.

Transfer the celeriac purée to a mixing bowl and whisk in the eggs, one by one. Now stir in the crème fraîche. Season with salt and pepper.

Grease the insides of 4 individual ramekin dishes with butter. Sprinkle the cornflour over the base and sides of each dish and tap off the excess. Divide the mixture among the dishes. Stand the ramekins in a bain-marie of hot water and bake in the heated oven for 25 minutes or until well-risen and golden-brown.

Meanwhile, prepare the carrot butter: peel and wash the carrots. Slice them thinly and boil them in salted water for 20 minutes. Reserve 4 large carrot slices to decorate the ramekins and purée the rest in a blender until very smooth.

Bring 4 tablespoons of water to the boil in a small saucepan. Cut the butter into small pieces and whisk it, a piece at a time, into the hot water. Add the carrot purée and the chives. Return the sauce to the boil for a few seconds. Check the seasoning.

To serve the *mousseline*: turn out each ramekin on to an individual plate and decorate with the remaining carrot slices. Carefully spoon the carrot butter around the *mousseline*. Serve at once.

*Root vegetables on the garden path*

## *Pintade Rôtie aux Cœurs de Laitue*

ROAST GUINEA-FOWL WITH LETTUCE HEARTS

2 petit suisse cheeses
salt and pepper
½ teaspoon chopped tarragon
½ teaspoon chopped chives
1 guinea-fowl (1.5 kg / 3 lb)
1 carrot, chopped
1 shallot, chopped
1 stick celery, chopped
100 g / 4 oz bacon, cubed into lardons
50 g / 2 oz sultanas
2 tablespoons port
8 small lettuce hearts
50 g / 2 oz butter
150 g / 5 oz pickling onions
250 ml / 8 fl oz chicken stock
1 bouquet garni

*Serves 6*

In a mixing bowl, mash the petit suisse cheeses together with salt, pepper and the herbs. Spoon this mixture inside the guinea-fowl and sew up the vent with kitchen thread.

Preheat the oven to 220°C / 425°F / gas mark 7.

Place the guinea-fowl in an earthenware baking dish and cook for 30 minutes in the heated oven, basting from time to time. Spoon the carrot, shallot, celery and lardons around the bird, mix well with the cooking juices and cook for a further 35 minutes or until the guinea-fowl is cooked through and tender.

Meanwhile, soak the sultanas in the port. Wash and dry the lettuce hearts. Heat half the butter in a cast-iron deep pan or flameproof casserole and gently sweat the lettuce hearts and pickling onions until transparent and limp. Add the stock, bouquet garni, salt and pepper. Lay a sheet of buttered greaseproof paper over the vegetables. Cover and simmer over a very low heat for 30 minutes, making sure there are 2–3 tablespoons of cooking juices left in the pan.

When the guinea-fowl is cooked, remove from the oven and keep warm while you prepare the sauce.

Lift the lettuce hearts from the pan with a slotted spoon and keep warm. Skim the excess fat from the roasting pan and pour in the lettuce stock. Bring to the boil, scraping the cooking juices from the roasting pan. Add the soaked sultanas and check the seasoning. Reduce the sauce until syrupy and pour into a gravy-boat. Carve the guinea-fowl on to a serving platter. Serve surrounded by the braised lettuce hearts.

## *Spaghetti aux Courgettes*

SPAGHETTI WITH COURGETTES

500 g / 1 lb fresh spaghetti
1 teaspoon olive oil
6 medium courgettes, sliced but not peeled
2 large garlic cloves
1 tablespoon finely chopped chives
125 ml / 4 fl oz crème fraîche
25 g / 1 oz butter
salt and pepper
a few walnut kernels

*Serves 4–6*

Cook the spaghetti in plenty of boiling salted water with the olive oil for 5 minutes. Blanch the courgettes and garlic in salted water for 5 minutes – they must remain slightly crunchy.

Drain the pasta and courgettes well, then mix together in a shallow serving dish. Keep warm.

Heat the crème fraîche and butter with the chives, salt and pepper. Stir well and pour over the pasta. Decorate with walnut kernels and serve at once.

## *Confit de Pommes aux Pruneaux*

BAKED APPLES AND PRUNES

This healthy dessert needs to be prepared a day in advance. No spice is added, to retain the full flavour of freshly picked fragrant apples.

100 g / 4 oz sugar
250 ml / 8 fl oz water
250 g / 9 oz prunes
500 g / 1 lb dessert apples
25 g / 1 oz unsalted butter

*Serves 6*

Preheat the oven to 190°C / 375°F / gas mark 5.

Put the sugar and water into a large saucepan and cook, stirring, until the sugar is dissolved and the liquid is syrupy. Add the prunes. Simmer over a low heat until tender. Stone the prunes and pound them by hand to a pulp.

Butter a charlotte dish. Peel and core the apples carefully, leaving them whole. Slice thinly crosswise.

Place a layer of apples in the dish, then a layer of prunes, and so on, finishing with a layer of apples.

Bake in the heated oven for 45–50 minutes. Leave to cool, covered, at room temperature, then refrigerate overnight. Turn out on to a plate and serve with lightly whipped cream.

*An old family recipe: apple and prune mould*

# The Four Seasons Garden

*The orchard in spring*

It is late spring in the Drôme. The air is light and the cicadas remind us that we are just at the door of Provence.

In the kitchen garden, dwarf beans, broad beans and mange-tout peas are so young and tender that they will hardly need cooking.

In the *orangerie* which brightens up the otherwise austere outlook of the small château, lemons, nectarines, peppers, courgettes and cherry tomatoes have ripened in secret.

Yet tonight, with the mountain just behind us, it will be cold enough to hibernate by a log fire and resurrect winter recipes.

'I love this house,' says Anne. 'Because of its location, you can play with the four seasons, all in one day. You can flout nature or adjust to it, according to your mood.'

Anne proved her point with the food she served that day. We had a summery *cuisine minceur* luncheon which started with a light cold pepper stuffed with cottage cheese, coriander and olives. Then a very small helping of fresh tagliatelle mixed with young steamed vegetables and served with an amazing dish of cherry tomatoes sautéed with scented geranium leaves. We finished with a featherweight soufflé made with the lemons grown in the *orangerie*.

*Early nectarines have been picked in the orangerie*

After a long afternoon walk and as soon as the sun disappeared behind the mountain, the earth gently cooled down and the evening chill called for *soupe montagnarde* made with celeriac, mature Beaufort cheese and thick country bread. This was followed by a wild herb omelette and to finish, a laudable thin walnut tart.

The seasonal theme so close to Anne's heart was repeated in the décor of the house. The kitchen, which must have originally been the communal room of the house, had all the cosiness of winter: a huge fireplace fitted with an antique brass spit for slow roasting in the style of the region, deep leather armchairs which had seen better days and a huge chest filled with logs. The other rooms were a mixture of pastel shades with fruit and flower prints until one reached the cornucopia of summer in the *orangerie*.

It was a perfect evening. We sipped a *marc de Bourgogne*. 'Anything else?' asked Anne. 'Vivaldi, please,' I replied.

*Peppers: perfect for a light luncheon*

## LUNCH

### *Poivrons Froids Farcis*

COLD STUFFED PEPPERS

4 red peppers
2 eggs
16 black pitted olives
225 g / 8 oz fromage frais
1 teaspoon chopped tarragon
a few coriander leaves
1 large garlic clove, crushed
2 medium carrots
3 tablespoons olive oil
1 tablespoon wine vinegar
salt and pepper
coriander leaves, to garnish

*Serves 4–8*

Halve the peppers and discard the seeds. Blanch them for 10 minutes in boiling salted water. Drain well and pat dry with kitchen paper. Leave to cool.

Meanwhile, hard-boil the eggs, shell them and chop them roughly. Finely chop 8 of the olives.

In a bowl, mash the fromage frais with the herbs and garlic. Add the chopped eggs and the chopped olives. Peel and finely grate the carrots. Whisk together the oil and vinegar and season the carrots with this vinaigrette. Gently work the carrots into the cheese and egg mixture. Season with salt and pepper.

Spoon the mixture into the halved peppers. Garnish each one with a black olive and a coriander leaf. Served chilled.

### *Tagliatelle en Habit Vert aux Champignons*

MEDLEY OF GREEN VEGETABLES, MUSHROOMS AND NOODLES

200 g / 7 oz small French beans, topped and tailed
100 g / 4 oz young broad beans, shelled
150 g / 5 oz mange-tout, topped and tailed
2 small courgettes, sliced but not peeled
500 g / 1 lb tagliatelle
3 tablespoons olive oil
4 large mushrooms, sliced
1 small garlic clove, crushed
juice of 1 lemon
salt and pepper
100 g / 4 oz young spinach leaves
1 teaspoon chopped chives
1 teaspoon chopped chervil

*Serves 4*

Cook the French beans, broad beans and mange-tout in boiling salted water for 8 minutes. Cook the courgettes for 5 minutes in salted boiling water. Drain the vegetables and keep warm. Cook the tagliatelle until just tender.

Meanwhile, heat 1 tablespoon of the olive oil in a frying pan and sauté the mushrooms with the garlic over a medium heat without letting them take colour. Add the lemon juice, salt and pepper.

Drain the tagliatelle. Chop the spinach leaves very finely. Mix the warm tagliatelle with the spinach, French beans, broad beans, mange-tout and courgettes in a large shallow serving dish. Add the remaining olive oil and the chives and chervil. Mix well so that the flavours intermingle. Check the seasoning. Garnish with the sliced mushrooms and serve at once.

## Tomates Cerise aux Feuilles de Géranium Rose

CHERRY TOMATOES SAUTÉED WITH SCENTED GERANIUM LEAVES

500 g / 1 lb cherry tomatoes
2 tablespoons olive oil
3 scented geranium leaves
½ teaspoon sugar
salt and pepper
1 garlic clove, crushed
1 tablespoon chopped parsley

*Serves 4*

Wash and dry the tomatoes, leaving them whole. Heat the oil in a frying-pan, add the scented geranium leaves and simmer over a very low heat for 5–10 minutes to bring out the flavours. Discard the geranium leaves.

Increase the heat under the frying-pan and sauté the tomatoes in the flavoured oil, adding the sugar, salt, pepper and garlic. Shake the tomatoes in the pan until they start to caramelize, at the same time making sure they do not burn. Add the chopped parsley, stir and carefully spoon on to a serving dish decorated with fresh geranium leaves. Serve at once.

*The delicate flavour of geranium leaves with cherry tomatoes*

## *Soufflé au Citron*

LEMON SOUFFLÉ

10 large sugar lumps
1 lemon
½ teaspoon grated lemon zest
500 ml / 17 fl oz milk
1 tablespoon cornflour
3 eggs

*For the dish*
25 g / 1 oz butter
2 tablespoons caster sugar
icing sugar, to decorate

*Serves 4*

Preheat the oven to 200°C / 400°F / gas mark 6.

Rub the sugar with the lemon. Put the grated lemon zest into a saucepan with the milk. Bring the milk just to the boil, then remove from the heat and leave to cool and infuse.

When the milk is just tepid, stir in the cornflour, mixed to a smooth paste with a little of the milk. Return the pan to the heat and stir over a low heat for 5–6 minutes, until thickened. Remove from the heat and leave to cool.

Separate the eggs and place the whites in a deep mixing bowl.

When the lemon mixture has cooled, whisk in the egg yolks, one by one. Whisk the egg whites until stiff and fold delicately into the lemon mixture.

Grease a large soufflé dish with butter and sprinkle with sugar. Tap the dish to remove the excess. Pour the soufflé mixture into the dish and bake in the heated oven for 20–25 minutes or until the soufflé is well risen and golden-brown on top. Sprinkle with icing sugar and serve at once from the soufflé dish.

# DINNER

## *Soupe Montagnarde*

CELERIAC AND CHEESE SOUP

1 large head of celeriac
3 leeks
2 large carrots
1 large onion
50 g / 2 oz butter
3 large potatoes
1 litre / 1¾ pints chicken stock
salt and pepper
2 tablespoons thick crème fraîche
a pinch of freshly grated nutmeg
1 tablespoon finely chopped chervil, to garnish

*For the croûtes*
6 slices of French bread
25 g / 1 oz butter
150 g / 5 oz Beaufort cheese, thinly sliced

*Serves 6*

Peel and dice the celeriac. Trim the leeks and discard the toughest outer leaves, leaving as much tender green as possible. Peel the carrots. Wash the leeks and carrots carefully under cold running water and slice them downwards and across into oblong pieces. Peel and thinly slice the onion.

Place the butter in a large saucepan, cover with the vegetables and leave to sweat over a low heat, stirring from time to time, until the celeriac and carrots are almost tender. Meanwhile, peel and dice the potatoes. Pour the stock over the vegetables, then add the diced potatoes. Season with salt and pepper. Cover and simmer for 35–40 minutes or until the vegetables are cooked.

Preheat the oven to 230°C / 450°F / gas mark 8.

Make the croûtes: spread the bread slices with the butter. Toast the buttered bread in the oven until crisp and brown.

To serve: place the toasted bread at the bottom of a large soup tureen and top each slice with the cheese. Add the crème fraîche and nutmeg to the soup. Check the seasoning. Pour the soup over the cheese croûtes. Sprinkle with the chervil. Serve at once, before the bread becomes too soggy.

## *Omelette aux Herbes Folles*

POTATO AND MIXED HERB OMELETTE

2 tablespoons olive oil
4 potatoes, peeled and finely diced
8 eggs
1 garlic clove, crushed
a handful of freshly gathered mixed herbs: chervil, sweet marjoram, chives, basil, parsley
2 small spring onions, finely chopped
salt and pepper

*Serves 4*

Heat the oil in a large omelette pan. Sauté the potatoes until they are well coated with the oil. Lower the heat, cover the pan and cook the potatoes until tender and golden-brown.

Meanwhile, beat the eggs in a bowl, adding the garlic, mixed herbs and spring onions.

Uncover the pan, turn up the heat and pour the egg mixture over the potatoes. When the under part of the omelette begins to set, make a few slits at the surface with a wooden spatula, tilting the pan slightly so that the uncooked liquid may set as well. Cook until the underneath is golden-brown, leaving the surface of the omelette moist. Season with salt and freshly ground black pepper. Fold in half on to a heated serving plate and serve at once.

## *Tarte aux Noix*

WALNUT TART

*For the pastry*
225 g / 8 oz plain flour
a pinch of salt
2 egg yolks
75 g / 3 oz caster sugar
150 g / 5 oz unsalted butter, softened

*For the filling*
200 g / 7 oz walnut kernels
2 eggs
1 egg yolk
100 g / 4 oz caster sugar
100 g / 4 oz unsalted butter, melted
1 tablespoon single cream

*Serves 4*

Sift the flour and salt into a mixing bowl and make a well in the centre. Add the egg yolks, sugar and butter and, with cool fingertips, work the egg, sugar and butter together, then gradually draw in the flour until a soft dough is formed. Roll out the pastry immediately and use to line a 30-cm / 12-inch tart tin. Chill for 30 minutes.

Carefully halve the walnut kernels.

Preheat the oven to 190°C / 375°F / gas mark 5.

Make the filling: using an electric whisk, cream together the eggs and egg yolk with the sugar until creamy, then whisk in the melted butter and the cream. Stir in the walnut kernels and pour the mixture on to the chilled dough. Bake in the heated oven for 25–30 minutes or until the filling is set and slightly caramelized. Serve lukewarm or cold.

*Walnuts stored with the garden tools*

# The Water Garden

At the heart of the Northern city of Amiens, just a step away from the cathedral, leeks, cabbages and all the Northern root vegetables grow in the biggest canal-irrigated gardens of France: Les Hortillonnages.

The gardens can only be reached by punt, through fens and dykes. Some are used by market gardeners, but a few are privately owned.

Margot and her husband live in a small brick house with an ornamental garden, but since she inherited her father's plot in this Venice of the North, she punts daily among herons, grebes and all kinds of waterfowl to tend the land. She has mixed flowers with the vegetables, mainly marigolds to prevent insects. Large, bright irises grow along the water's edge, mingling with the flowers of the beans and peas. Produce is kept green by the constant humidity.

In the kitchen we unload leeks, onions and potatoes, and tiny carrots which will be braised in butter and sage to accompany grilled meat. The first course is a recipe created by Margot for her daughter's engagement: instead of the usual regional leek tart, she makes individual *millefeuille*, in which leeks and Mornay sauce are layered between sheets of puff pastry.

With the grilled pork chops she has served the local onion sauce – *sauce soubise.* Dessert is a light orange mousse laced with Grand Marnier.

*Fens and dykes surround the gardens*

## Lunch

# *Millefeuille de Poireaux*

LEEKS AND HAM IN FEATHERWEIGHT PUFF PASTRY

*For the pastry*
200 g / 7 oz strong white flour
a pinch of salt
150 g / 5 oz good unsalted butter
125 ml / 4 fl oz iced water
1 egg yolk, to glaze

*For the filling*
1 kg / 2 lb leeks
1 onion
50 g / 2 oz butter
1 bay leaf
salt and pepper

*Leeks and potatoes*

*For the Mornay sauce*
300 ml / 10 fl oz milk
25 g / 1 oz butter
1 heaped tablespoon plain flour
100 g / 4 oz Gruyère cheese, grated
salt and pepper
a pinch of freshly grated nutmeg
8 thin slices of cooked ham

*Serves 6*

Preheat the oven to 220°C / 425°F / gas mark 7.

With the pastry ingredients, make a *pâte feuilletée* according to the instructions on page 94. Roll the pastry out on a lightly floured wooden board to the width and length of your baking sheet. The pastry should be no more than 3 mm / ⅛ inch thick. Place on the baking sheet and brush the surface with the egg yolk mixed with a little water. Bake in the heated oven for 25 minutes or until well puffed and golden-brown. While still warm, slice the pastry horizontally into 2 layers and transfer both sheets to cool on a pastry rack.

Meanwhile, make the filling: trim the leeks and discard the toughest outer leaves, leaving as much green as possible. Wash the leeks carefully under cold running water and slice them downwards and across into small oblong pieces. Peel and thinly slice the onion. Put the butter into a saucepan, cover with the leeks and onions, add the bay leaf, salt and pepper and cook, uncovered, over a low heat until the vegetables are tender and the cooking liquid has evaporated. Discard the bay leaf and set the saucepan aside.

Make a thick Mornay sauce: scald the milk in a saucepan. Melt the butter in a heavy-based saucepan, stir in the flour and cook for 1–2 minutes. Gradually work in the hot milk, stirring constantly to avoid lumps. Cook the sauce, stirring, over the lowest possible heat, until well thickened (it should be of a

spreading consistency). Stir in 75 g / 3 oz of the grated cheese, with salt, pepper and nutmeg.

Spread the sauce over one pastry sheet, reserving 2 tablespoons to be mixed with the leeks. Lay the ham over the sauce and cover with the second sheet of pastry. Mix the leeks with the remaining Mornay sauce. Carefully spoon over the pastry and leave to cool.

Using a long serrated knife, divide the *millefeuille* into 6 equal portions. Sprinkle each one with the remaining grated cheese. Warm up in a hot oven just before serving.

*The kitchen garden*

*Carrots in a bowl*

## Carottes Picardes à la Sauge

CARROTS BRAISED WITH SAGE

750 g / 1½ lb carrots
50 g / 2 oz butter
2 teaspoons plain flour
600 ml / 1 pint chicken stock
1 bay leaf
3 sage leaves
1 teaspoon crème fraîche

*Serves 6*

Peel and wash the carrots. Cut them into thin slices. Melt the butter in a heavy-based saucepan and sauté the carrots. Sprinkle with the flour, mix well and add the stock, bay leaf, sage, salt and pepper. Cover, reduce the heat to simmering point and cook for 35–40 minutes or until the carrots are tender.

To serve: check the seasoning, discard the bay leaf, and mix the crème fraîche into the sauce.

## Soubise Picarde

ONION SAUCE

500 g / 1 lb large onions
50 g / 2 oz butter
1 tablespoon plain flour
150 ml / 5 fl oz chicken stock
1 teaspoon malt vinegar
a pinch of freshly grated nutmeg
1 bay leaf
salt and pepper
2 teaspoons crème fraîche

*Serves 6*

Peel and thinly slice the onions. Melt the butter in a heavy-based saucepan over a medium heat and sprinkle with the flour, stirring constantly. Add a little water and stir well until a smooth paste is obtained.

Add the onions, mix well and pour in the stock. Add the vinegar, nutmeg, bay leaf, salt and pepper. Simmer, uncovered, over the lowest heat, stirring from time to time until the onions are soft and the mixture creamy. Add a little extra stock if necessary.

Discard the bay leaf. Purée the onions with a fork, work in the crème fraîche and check the seasoning. Pour into a sauce-boat to serve.

## *Mousse à l'Orange*

ORANGE MOUSSE

juice of 5 oranges
1 teaspoon finely grated orange rind
150 g / 5 oz caster sugar
6 egg yolks
1 tablespoon Grand Marnier
4 egg whites

*Serves 6*

In a mixing bowl, pour the orange juice and rind over the sugar and whisk to a paste. Then whisk in the egg yolks, one by one. Transfer the mixture to a double saucepan or a heatproof bowl set over a pan of barely simmering water and stir constantly until thickened. Remove from the heat and add the Grand Marnier. Leave to cool.

Whisk the egg whites until stiff and fold them delicately into the orange mixture. Spoon into individual serving dishes or ramekins and keep chilled over a bed of ice-cubes until ready to serve.

*The gardens can only be reached by boat*

# The Riverside Allotments

*Will this Swiss chard win the prize?*

In the riverside city of Angers, in the Loire Valley, there are no fewer than 1500 allotments. When I visited Monsieur de la Celle, president of the horticultural society for the region, we agreed that no book should be written about the *potagers* of France without mentioning the kitchen gardens of the city-dwellers.

'The institutional allotment, founded towards the end of the nineteenth century, was first created to help the factory worker feed his family, to give him the opportunity to escape the miasma of an often sordid home for a few hours and to stop him sinking into despair and alcoholism,' says Monsieur de la Celle. 'Since then, of course,' he adds, 'social attitudes have changed and today the allotment is simply the garden offered to any flat-dweller who wishes to grow vegetables. There are none the less certain rules,' he continues. 'For example, although flowers are allowed, at least fifteen species of vegetable have to be grown in each plot, and every year we have a competition for the best-kept garden and, of course, *le mouton à cinq pattes*, the fun competition for the biggest vegetable of each variety.'

*Many good recipes will be exchanged over a glass of wine*

Early one Saturday morning I followed Monsieur Vaugondry, president of the allotments' association in Angers, who himself has an allotment, to a delightful sight. Men were digging, women were gathering the fruits of their husbands' efforts. It was a mixture of good humour, serious bartering of seeds or cuttings, happy meetings under the vine-clad huts for morning coffee breaks – unless more potent beverages were offered.

I gleaned some especially interesting cooking ideas, for people here are from different areas of France, and so tend to grow the indigenous plants of their native region, which are put to excellent use in their wives' recipes.

By 11 o'clock I was happily drinking chilled *vin d'Anjou* with the Janin family. Madame Janin had brought a terrine of *pâté de lapin fermière* to go with it: a moist rabbit pâté, very lean and easy to prepare.

Later on, I was to learn the secrets of a *velouté* of Brussels sprouts, a creamy soup which sounded different and seducing and one that is definitely worth trying.

Madame Acker from Alsace gave me two fine recipes: one for chicken Alsacienne braised with sausages, juniper berries, cabbage and root vegetables; the other, an unusual plum tart which is a delight.

Vin de Table
Les Vieux Papes

*More than a hundred gardens are gathered here*

My favourite recipe, however, which I often cook now at home, was given to me by Madame Lemière. It is a *tourte de carottes en robe de chou* – a mixture of minced carrots, leeks, onions and turnips baked briefly inside young cabbage leaves. Served with a cream and herb sauce, it makes a wonderful main course.

I was not allowed to leave without giving one of my own recipes. I chose my mother's version of our Norman *tarte aux pommes,* the lightest and tastiest apple tart I have ever come across.

## Lunch

### Pâté de Lapin Fermière au Vin de Loire

POTTED RABBIT IN ANJOU WINE

*For the marinade*
1 large oven-ready rabbit
3 onions, sliced
2 garlic cloves
1 carrot, sliced
2 cloves
salt and pepper
1 large bouquet garni
250 ml / 8 fl oz dry Anjou white wine

*'Flowers are allowed ...'*

*For the pâté*
225 g / 8 oz lean veal, cubed
225 g / 8 oz lean pork, cubed
225 g / 8 oz coarsely minced belly of pork
1 bouquet garni
2 garlic cloves, unpeeled
200 ml / 7 fl oz dry white Anjou wine
50 ml / 2 fl oz Cognac
salt and pepper

*Serves 8*

Place the whole rabbit in a large earthenware dish. Place the vegetables and bouquet garni around it. Pour in the wine. Leave to marinate in a cold room for 3 days, turning the rabbit from time to time.

Preheat the oven to 150°C / 300°F / gas mark 2.

To make the pâté: dry the rabbit with kitchen paper and joint it. Place the rabbit pieces in a large casserole together with the veal, pork and minced belly of pork. Push the bouquet garni and garlic into the centre of the dish. Pour the wine and Cognac over the meat and season well with salt and coarsely ground black pepper. Cover tightly and bake in the heated oven for 2½–3 hours or until the meat comes off the rabbit bones.

Carefully discard the bones and the bouquet garni. Mix the three meats together with a fork and pack tightly into a large china terrine. Bring the cooking juices to the boil and leave to reduce slightly. Check the seasoning and pour the stock over the meat. Chill until set firm. This pâté will keep for a week in the refrigerator.

## Tourte de Carottes en Robe de Chou

CARROT AND CABBAGE CAKE

7 large cabbage leaves
4 large carrots
3 baby turnips
3 onions
1 small garlic clove
1 small bunch of parsley
3 young leeks
175 g / 6 oz butter
salt and pepper
3 large eggs, beaten

*For the sauce*
25 g / 1 oz butter
225 ml / 8 fl oz crème fraîche
2 heaped teaspoons chopped chives
salt and pepper

*Serves 6*

Carefully wash the cabbage leaves. Blanch them for 3 minutes in boiling salted water, then immediately run them under the cold tap. Pat dry between two sheets of kitchen paper.

Trim, peel and wash the carrots and turnips. Grate them finely in a food processor. Chop the onions, garlic, parsley and leeks.

Melt 100 g / 4 oz of the butter in a large heavy-based saucepan and sweat all the vegetables over a very low heat for 15 minutes, stirring from time to time. Season with salt and pepper. Set aside to cool slightly, then stir in the beaten eggs.

Preheat the oven to 190°C / 375°F / gas mark 5.

Generously grease a round deep cake tin with some of the remaining butter. Line the tin with the cabbage leaves, overlapping the edge of the tin. Spoon in the vegetable and egg mixture. Fold the cabbage leaves over the top and place an extra one over the surface, if necessary. Dot with the remaining butter, cover loosely with a piece of kitchen foil and bake in the heated oven for 20 minutes or until a skewer inserted into the middle comes out clean.

Meanwhile, make the sauce: melt the butter with the crème fraîche over a low heat, add the chives and season to taste with salt and pepper.

To serve: turn the vegetable mould on to a heated round serving platter. Serve cut into slices, with the sauce passed separately in a sauce-boat.

*Light carrot terrine, to be served with a chive-flavoured cream sauce*

## Velouté de Choux de Bruxelle

CREAM OF BRUSSELS SPROUTS SOUP

750 g / 1¼ lb Brussels sprouts
2 medium potatoes
2 onions
60 g / 2½ oz butter
750 ml / 1¼ pints chicken stock
2 tablespoons crème fraîche
2 teaspoons chopped chives
1 teaspoon chopped chervil

*To serve*
100 g / 4 oz smoked bacon, cubed into lardons
1 teaspoon chopped parsley

*Serves 6*

Wash the Brussels sprouts and discard the toughest outer leaves. Blanch the sprouts for 10 minutes in plenty of boiling salted water. Drain well.

Peel and dice the potatoes, peel and slice the onions.

Melt 50 g / 2½ oz of the butter in a flameproof casserole and cook the onions until they are transparent and limp, making sure they do not brown at all. Pour in the stock and add the potatoes and Brussels sprouts. Cover, lower the heat and simmer for 40 minutes.

Blend the soup to a smooth purée in a blender. Return the soup to the pan and add the crème fraîche, chives, chervil and the remaining butter. Reheat gently, stirring from time to time.

Meanwhile, fry the lardons in a non-stick frying pan, until crisp. Chop them as finely as possible and put them in a small serving bowl. Sprinkle the lardons with the parsley.

Pour the soup into a tureen and serve piping hot, accompanied by the bacon lardons.

*The garden shed*

## Poulet Braisé à l'Alsacienne

CHICKEN BRAISED IN THE STYLE OF ALSACE

2 tablespoons sunflower oil
1 garlic clove, chopped
2 shallots, chopped
1 teaspoon powdered bay leaf
2 teaspoons juniper berries, crushed
salt and pepper
50 g / 2 oz butter
1 free-range chicken (1.5 kg / 3 lb)
1 carrot, diced
2 onions, sliced
2 leeks, trimmed
2 baby turnips, sliced
1 small cabbage, quartered
1 large smoked sausage
300 ml / 10 fl oz chicken stock
125 ml / 4 fl oz Alsace white wine

*Serves 6*

The day before, combine 1 tablespoon of the oil with the garlic, shallots, bay leaf, juniper berries and pepper. Place the chicken in a bowl and rub the spice mixture all over it, inside and outside. Cover loosely and keep refrigerated.

Preheat the oven to 180°C / 350°F / gas mark 4.

Heat the remaining oil and the butter in a flameproof casserole and sauté the spiced chicken until golden-brown on all sides. Remove the chicken and set aside. Add the carrot, onions, leeks and turnips to the casserole. Mix well and sauté until the onions are transparent.

Return the chicken to the casserole with the vegetables and surround it with the pieces of cabbage and the sausage cut into large chunks.

Pour the stock and wine over the meat, cover and cook in the heated oven for 1½ hours or until the chicken is well cooked.

To serve: take the bird out of the casserole. Carve and transfer to a heated shallow serving platter. Arrange the vegetables and sausage around the chicken and spoon the cooking juices over the whole dish. Serve at once.

## Tarte aux Quetsches

VICTORIA PLUM TART

*For the pastry*
225 g / 8 oz plain flour
100 g / 4 oz unsalted butter
a pinch of salt
3 tablespoons iced water

*For the filling*
4 sponge fingers
100 g / 4 oz ground almonds
a pinch of ground cinnamon
a pinch of freshly grated nutmeg
½ teaspoon finely grated lemon zest
1.5 kg / 3 lb plums
100 g / 4 oz caster sugar
50 g / 2 oz unsalted butter

*Serves 6*

Prepare the pastry as described opposite.

Grind the sponge fingers in a blender. Stir in the ground almonds, cinnamon, nutmeg and lemon zest.

Halve the plums and discard the stones.

Roll out the pastry and use to line a 30-cm / 12-inch tart dish. Sprinkle the spiced biscuit and almond crumbs over the dough. Arrange the plums on top, standing them close together, pointed ends up. Sprinkle with the sugar. Dot with the butter cut into small pieces and bake in the heated oven for 40 minutes. Serve lukewarm or cold.

## Tarte Fine Aux Pommes

APPLE TART

*For the pastry*
225 g / 8 oz plain flour
a pinch of salt
150 g / 5 oz unsalted butter
iced water

*For the filling*
6–8 fragrant dessert apples
1 teaspoon grated lemon zest
2 tablespoons soft brown sugar
75 g / 3 oz top-quality unsalted butter

*Serves 6*

To make the pastry: sift the flour and salt on to a large wooden board. Dot the butter, cut into small pieces, over the flour. With cool fingertips, working quickly, rub the butter into the flour and gradually add the iced water until a smooth dough has been obtained. Roll out immediately very thinly and use to line a 30-cm / 12-inch tart dish. Refrigerate for 15–20 minutes.

Preheat the oven to 200°C / 400°F / gas mark 6.

Peel and core the apples and slice them thinly. Arrange them over the dough in a circular pattern, overlapping, mounding them up slightly in the centre. Sprinkle the fruit with the lemon zest, then with the sugar. Dot all over with the butter cut into tiny squares and bake for 25–30 minutes in the heated oven. Eat warm or cold but do not reheat.

*Questche, an indigenous French plum*

# Grand'-mère's Store Cupboard

*The manor house by the sea near Barfleur*

When I arrived at the small manor-house by the sea, near Barfleur, a child opened the door. His teeth were embedded in an enormous slice of bread and jam; all I could see of his face were two huge smiling brown eyes.

'Come in,' said a soft woman's voice, 'and join us for breakfast.'

Claudette was feeding her youngest grandchild. There were a few seconds of French formality from her, such as, 'I'm sorry I was not able to answer the door myself,' followed by 'Laelian, could you please go and wash your sticky hands before you shake hands with Madame Tilleray'... too late, Laelian's huge brown eyes smiled again as he smeared rhubarb jam all over my right palm.

'Mamie never stops making jam,' he said, adding, 'and I grow the best *patates'* (a slang word for potatoes). Formality soon gave way to cheerful conviviality and I promised to go and admire the prized spuds as soon as I had finished my coffee.

In fact, since entering the kitchen I had been unable to take my eyes off an antique cupboard packed with jam jars, large and small, preserving bottles and decanters obviously containing home-made liqueurs . . . the epitome of the well-organized Frenchwoman's store cupboard.

*The cupboard, always stocked with home-made treats*

Claudette explained that the cupboard was in fact the most sentimental heirloom she possessed and that she felt it was right to fill it with the homely preserves she is so fond of making. 'We call it *le buffet de la grand'-mère*, as it belonged to my mother,' she said, 'and everyone in the family knows that it is always full of home-made treats and goodies.'

As we stepped outside, I took one look at the kitchen garden and understood that Mamie's hobbies obviously included gardening as well as jam-making. The manor-house to which Claudette and her husband retired a few years back is built on an ancient hill facing the sea and it is Claudette who restored the terraced garden with a mixture of fruit trees, shrubs, rhododendrons, daisies and all kinds of soft fruit. Each grandchild is allowed his small vegetable plot and Laelian knowingly told me that it was a little early to dig his potatoes but that his courgettes had fed the whole family the previous night.

Before returning to the kitchen to discuss recipes, we passed the pond by which hens, geese and ducks were warming themselves in the early summer sun.

## Marmelade de Carottes Citronnée

CARROT AND LEMON JAM

2 kg / 4 lb young carrots
1.5 kg / 3 lb preserving sugar
finely grated zest of 1 large lemon
½ teaspoon ground cinnamon

Peel and wash the carrots. Cut them into even slices and cook in boiling water until tender. Drain well and purée in a blender. Mix the lemon zest with the carrot pulp. Transfer to a preserving pan. Add the sugar, cinnamon and a little water. Cook slowly over a low heat, stirring often, for about 30 minutes or until the jam reaches setting-point. Transfer to sterilized jars and seal well.

*A bouquet from the vegetable garden*

## Confiture de Cerises aux Groseilles

CHERRY AND REDCURRANT PRESERVE

1 kg / 2 lb redcurrants
2 tablespoons water
2 kg / 4 lb cherries, stoned
2.5 kg / 4½ lb preserving sugar

Place the redcurrants in a large saucepan with the water. Bring to the boil to let the fruit burst. Immediately remove from the heat and strain through a jelly bag. Transfer the redcurrant juice to a preserving pan and add the cherries and sugar. Bring to the boil, stirring well, and leave to boil for 2 minutes. Remove from the heat and leave to stand for 5 minutes.

Bring the mixture back to the boil for another 2 minutes, again remove from the heat and leave to stand for 5 minutes. Repeat the process twice more. Spoon the cherries into sterilized jars. Bring the syrup back to the boil until it reaches setting-point. Pour over the cherries and seal the jars well.

## Confiture de Poires

PEAR JAM

2 kg / 4 lb pears
juice of 1 lemon
1.6 kg / 3¼ lb preserving sugar
3 tablespoons water

Peel and slice the pears. Sprinkle them with lemon juice and layer the fruit in a large bowl, adding some sugar between each layer. Leave in a cool place, covered with a tea-towel, for 12 hours, in order to draw out the juices.

Transfer to a preserving pan and add the water. Bring to the boil, stirring gently. Lower the heat slightly and cook for 30 minutes or until the jam reaches setting-point. To test for setting-point, pour a teaspoon of the hot jam on to a chilled saucer: the jam is ready if a skin forms on the surface – test with your finger. Transfer the jam to sterilized jam jars and seal well.

## *Gelée de Groseilles à l'Ancienne*

OLD-FASHIONED REDCURRANT JELLY

1 kg / 2 lb redcurrants
500 g / 1 lb whitecurrants
500 g / 1 lb raspberries
preserving sugar (500 g / 1 lb per 600 ml / 1 pint juice)

Using a fork, carefully strip the currants off their stems. Transfer the redcurrants, whitecurrants and raspberries to a preserving pan and add a tumbler of water. Cook over a high heat until the fruit bursts, stirring with a spoon.

Remove the pan from the heat and leave to cool, then strain the fruit through a jelly bag into a large bowl. This will take several hours.

Measure the juice back into the rinsed-out pan. For every 600 ml / 1 pint of juice, add 500 g / 1 lb of preserving sugar. Stir over a gentle heat until the sugar has completely dissolved. Turn up the heat and boil for 10 minutes or until the jelly reaches setting-point. Pour into sterilized jam jars. The following day, cover with discs of waxed paper and seal.

## *Gelée de Tomates au Géranium Rose*

RED TOMATO AND SCENTED GERANIUM JELLY

2 kg / 4 lb ripe tomatoes
6 scented geranium leaves
preserving sugar (500 g / 1 lb per 600 ml / 1 pint juice)
1 vanilla pod, halved lengthways

Wash the tomatoes and cut them into chunks. Transfer them to a large saucepan, add the geranium leaves and cook with a little water until tender. Remove the pan from the heat. Leave to cool, then strain through a jelly bag into a large bowl.

Measure the juice back into the rinsed-out pan. For every 600 ml / 1 pint of juice add 500 g / 1 lb of preserving sugar, together with the vanilla pod. Stir over a low heat until the sugar has dissolved. Turn up the heat and boil for 10 minutes until the jelly reaches setting-point. Discard the vanilla pod. Pour into sterilized jam jars. The following day, cover with discs of waxed paper and seal. Serve with sponge cake.

## *Beurre de Pommes*

APPLE CURD

2 kg / 4 lb tart apples
600 ml / 1 pint sweet cider
1 kg / 2 lb soft brown sugar
1 cinnamon stick
1 vanilla pod, halved lengthways
zest of 1 lemon
4 cloves
75 ml / 3 fl oz Calvados

Wash but do not peel the apples and cut them into even pieces, leaving the pips. Place them in a large enamelled pan. Cover with the cider and simmer over a low heat for 25–30 minutes, stirring from time to time, until tender.

When the apples are cooked, discard the pips and purée the fruit in a blender. Weigh the pulp, then return it to the rinsed-out pan and add half its weight in sugar. Tie the cinnamon stick, vanilla pod, lemon zest and cloves up in a small piece of muslin and dip the bag into the centre of the pan. Cook for 4 hours over the lowest heat. The apple curd is ready when a small amount dropped on a plate does not run when you tilt the plate to one side.

Discard the spices and pour into air-tight jars. Heat the Calvados in a small pan, set it alight and pour it while flaming on top of the apple curd. Seal the jars at once. Store in a cold dark room.

*Preserves and harvest in the fruitier*

## *Cerises à l'Eau-de-vie*

CHERRIES IN *EAU-DE-VIE*

1 kg / 2 lb cherries
1 cinnamon stick
a pinch of ground mace
2 cloves
200 g / 7 oz sugar
300 ml / 10 fl oz *eau-de-vie*

Wash the cherries and dry them in a tea-cloth. Trim the stems, leaving only a short length. Place the cherries in a large jar. Add the spices and the sugar. Gradually pour in the *eau-de-vie* until it covers the fruit. Seal the jar tightly. The following day, shake the jar to make sure all the sugar has dissolved. Leave for at least 2 months in a cool dark room before serving.

## *Crème de Cassis*

BLACKCURRANT LIQUEUR

1 kg / 2 lb blackcurrants
12 blackcurrant leaves
1 cinnamon stick
1 clove
1 litre / 1¾ pints *eau-de-vie*
800 g / 1¾ lb sugar

Using a fork, carefully strip the currants off their stems. Wash them and gently pat dry with kitchen paper. Put the fruit into a jar and pound with a pestle.

Wash and dry the blackcurrant leaves. Place them in the base of a large bowl with the cinnamon and clove. Pour over the *eau-de-vie*.

Add the blackcurrants to the *eau-de-vie* and leaves and add the sugar. Stir well until all the sugar has dissolved. Pour the mixture into a large jar. Seal tightly and leave to macerate for a month at room temperature, preferably exposed to the sunlight. Then strain through a jelly bag, squeezing out as much of the juice as possible.

To bottle the *crème de cassis*: pour the liquid through a coffee filter into a bottle or decanter. This liqueur will keep for months.

## *Cornichons*

FRENCH PICKLED GHERKINS

1 kg / 2 lb small gherkins (pickling cucumbers)
coarse sea salt
24 pickling onions
2 cloves
a pinch of cayenne pepper
12 black peppercorns
2 garlic cloves
4 stems tarragon
1.5 litres / 2½ pints white wine vinegar

Wash and dry the gherkins, then layer them in a mixing bowl with salt. Leave the gherkins to marinate overnight to extract the juices. The following day, drain and dry them on kitchen paper without rinsing off the salt.

Place the gherkins in a large earthenware jar together with the other ingredients.

Bring the vinegar to the boil and immediately pour over the gherkins. Leave to macerate for 24 hours.

Then strain the vinegar into a saucepan and add an extra 200 ml / 7 fl oz fresh vinegar. Bring back to the boil, then pour over the gherkins. Cover tightly and leave for at least 6 weeks before serving sliced with drinks or as part of mixed hors-d'œuvre.

*A medley of flavours for afternoon tea*

## *Prunes au Vinaigre*

PICKLED PLUMS

1 kg / 2 lb firm plums
4 stems tarragon
1 litre / 1¾ pints sherry vinegar
2 tablespoons clear honey
½ teaspoon allspice
6 cloves
1 teaspoon green peppercorns
½ teaspoon freshly ground black pepper
a pinch of salt

Clean the plums and pat them dry. Place in a pickling jar and add the tarragon stems. Put the vinegar into a saucepan with the other ingredients and bring to the boil. Pour over the plums. Seal tightly. Leave to macerate for a month, away from direct light. Serve with *charcuterie*.

## *Raisins au Vinaigre*

PICKLED GRAPES

1 large bunch very green grapes
4 stems tarragon
6 cloves
1 teaspoon coriander seeds
1 teaspoon black peppercorns
1 litre / 1¾ pints wine vinegar
a pinch of salt

Detach the grapes from the stalk, wash and pat dry. Transfer to an earthenware or glass pickling jar and add tarragon stems. Bring the vinegar to the boil with the cloves, coriander seeds and peppercorns. Cover and leave to infuse for a few minutes. Pour the spiced liquid over the grapes. Leave to cool, then seal tightly. Leave to macerate for at least 2 weeks in a dry, cool room away from direct light.

## *Vin Blanc au Citron*

WHITE WINE WITH LEMON

2 litres / 3½ pints good white wine
200 g / 7 oz sugar
300 ml / 10 fl oz *eau-de-vie*
2 lemons, thickly sliced
3 cloves
1 vanilla pod, halved lengthways

Melt the sugar in the wine in a saucepan over a gentle heat. Pour into a large jar and add the *eau-de-vie*, lemons, cloves and vanilla pod. Cover well and leave to macerate for at least 2 days in a cold dark room. To serve, strain the liquid through a coffee filter. Serve well chilled.

## *Vin de Framboises*

RASPBERRY WINE

500 g / 1 lb raspberries
750 ml / 1¼ pints good claret
caster sugar (same weight as the juice obtained)

Pour the claret over the fruit in a tall glazed earthenware jar. Cover and leave to macerate in a cold dark place for a week. Strain through a jelly bag, squeezing out as much of the juice as possible. Measure the juice into a large saucepan and add the same weight in sugar. Stir over a gentle heat until the sugar has dissolved. Bring to the boil, then remove from the heat immediately. Leave to cool, then filter into sterilized bottles. Cork and serve, chilled, within a month.

*Prunes preserved in an eighteenth-century glass jar*

# List of Recipes

# Index

Page numbers referring to main recipes are in **bold**